He stands erect by bending over the fallen. He rises by lifting others. -Douglas Horton

BUILD A MAN:

A Mentorship Guide for Developing Men

Nicholas Robertson and Valentine Rodney

Edited by Danielle Brown- Robertson

Produce for IOBI-Excellence is not on Break.

BUILD A MAN: A MENTORSHIP GUIDE FOR DEVELOPING MEN (New Ed.) Copyright © 2023 by **Impact Online Institute Global.**

Published by:
Reason with Robdon

ISBN:978-1-990266-08-9

Book Cover Design by: **Iconic Presence**

- All rights reserved soley by the author. No part of the book may be reproduced, stored in a retreival system or transmitted by any means (mechanical, electronic, photocopy, recording or otherwise) without the written permission of the author.

- All scriptures are taken from the Holy Bible, New Living Translation, copyright ©1996, 2004, 2007 by the Tyndale House Foundation. Used by permission of Tyndale House Publishers Inc., Carol Stream, IL 30188. All rights reserved.

- All definitions are taken from Vine's Expository Dictionary of Old and New Testament Words, copyright © 1997 by Thomas Neilson, Inc. Used by permission of Thomas Neilson Inc., Nashville, Tennessee. All rights reserved.

IOBI instructors are available to speak and provide training at your conferences, workshops, crusades, conventions, seminars, youth ministry, mentorship, men's ministry, couple's ministry and any other ministry engagement.

School's Contact Details:

Email:	iobi@positivevibrationglobal.com
Website:	https://www.positivevibrationglobal.com/impact-online-bible-institute
Follow us: FB, IG, YT, Twitter	Reason with Robdon/ Impact Online Bible Institute/BuildAman Foundation Global

TABLE OF CONTENTS

INTRODUCTION

"Then the LORD God formed the man from the dust of the ground. He breathed the breath of life into the man's nostrils, and the man became a living person."

(Genesis 2: 7)

Most products today come with a user guide or instruction manual developed by the manufacturer to give a product description and other information regarding use and function of the product. One can choose to ignore the manual and attempt to by trial and error uncover how it functions. Not only is that method time consuming but you run the risk of potentially damaging the product because of a lack of qualified information. Reading and understanding the source document is integral to avoid what in some cases can be detrimental to the product. There is no need to operate in ignorance when the requisite information is available. You disregard the manual to your own peril.

The Bible is the ultimate manual that deals with the creation of man and provides critical information regarding his purpose. Most things in Genesis were created by the word of God (he spoke, and he saw), however the crowning glory of his creation was made from previously existing raw materials. God forming man from the dust of the ground is the clearest indication, that God chose to build the first man. God built the first man the original prototype fully mature, full functional and capable of managing His creation. All that the original man needed to be he knew. The man was not made like a robot but was given the power of choice. He could therefore of his own volition choose to do the right thing. He was built to last and to function in all is God ordained capacities.

The choice to disobey God put man into a tailspin and affected his ability to function as originally designed. The product was damaged and in need of restoration which was to eventually come in the person of Christ. Many male related issues are a consequence of the fall of man.

The depths of depravity and alienation from good may appear to be spiralling out of control but all is not lost. This book is intended to look at the original manual or user guide and to provide pertinent information that when applied will ultimately lead to restoration. The authors are well intentioned that instead of cursing the darkness we choose to light a candle to show the way.

'BuildAMan' has moved from an initiative or concept to the Genesis of what is expected to become a movement. We stand on the shoulders of our predecessors who have continually sought to address this critical issue within our various cultures. We choose to at this late hour to add our voices in the belief that change is not only possible it is inevitable, and we can salvage some good in the earth by the Grace of God. We have sought to contextualise the use of the manual to bring to the fore God's original design for man. It is our considered viewpoint that what is wrong with man can be fixed by what is right in scriptures.

The topics covered are by no means exhaustive but are presented with the view that if properly utilised can begin or continue the process towards building the man. It is going to take a collaborative effort to obtain maximum impact. Let us not be overwhelmed by the sheer magnitude of the task but let us get to work at once. We must first allow the manual to speak to us, then begin to appropriate the changes in our lives and by extension reach out to so many others in need of help.

The book you are holding in your hands is not just a product geared towards information but rather a tool for transformation. We begin with the question of identity clearly indicating that you were born a male, but you must become a man. You cannot become what you are ignorant of. Mans's identity is tied to his spirituality. You cannot be divorced or alienated from God and expect to become what is foundational to your design. The disconnect between man and God has opened a pandora's box type situation which can only be resolved by a return to the original purpose and intent. We have sought to address areas such as the man's interpersonal relationships, finances, sexuality, mentality, worth and ego to name a few. We are confident that the application of the truths uncovered in this book will help to further the conversation, strengthen the resolve and truly Build a Man.

MAN, AND HIS IDENTITY

"Know, first, who you are, and then adorn yourself accordingly."

<u>Epictetus</u>

One of the most productive revelations we can have, is understanding the man and his function, which will allow for a thorough examination of him and his identity. A conscientious analysis of the man and his identity will yield favourable answers to much-asked questions about his purpose, needs, responsibilities, and expectations. In this chapter, we will conduct an exhaustive investigation of the 'man' and his 'identity' in conjunction with God's plan for his life on earth.

Let us first examine the man as he was created and positioned by God.

Moses posits that "...God said, let us make man in our image, after our likeness: and let them have dominion over the fish of the sea, and over the fowl of the air, and over the cattle, and over all the earth, and over every creeping thing that creepeth upon the earth. ***(Genesis 1: 26)***

Words are the building blocks of sentences; therefore, a clear understanding of words will allow us to comprehend the message shared within its original context.

Let us unpack the word 'man' as intended within the text of reference.

The word 'man' is derived from the Hebrew word 'Adam,' meaning human beings and humankind. Therefore, the word 'Adam' here is plural and refers to both male and female.

So, God created man in His own image, in the image and likeness of God Male and female created he them; and blessed them, and called their name Adam, in the day when they were created. **(Genesis 5:2)**

We can cross-reference this understanding of 'Adam' being both male and female at creation in several scriptures within the Bible, including:

So, God created man in his own image, in the image of God created he him; male and female created he them. **(Genesis 1:27)**

The Bible makes a clear distinction between male and female. A man cannot be a woman neither can a woman be a man. It is God who determine our gender, not our emotions or social culture. Therefore, gender is not mutable.

And Adam said, this is now bone of my bones, and flesh of my flesh: she shall be called Woman, because she was taken out of Man. **(Genesis 2:23)**

The verse above shows an intelligible difference between man and woman regarding gender and sex by using two distinct words to represent each. The Hebrew word for a woman here is 'Ishshah,' distinguishing this specific creation from 'Iysh' the term used for man.

In another scripture the word 'Adam' refers to the first male (man) produced by God, the leader and steward of God's creation. He is the partner the woman and carrier of the seed, the genetic transporter of future offspring. He plays a key role in the reproductive process and cannot replaced.

And Adam said, this is now bone of my bones, and flesh of my flesh: she shall be called Woman, because she was taken out of Man. **(Genesis 2:23)**

We can insinuate from this scripture that Adam fully knew what God had made and presented (the newly constructed creation) was unique. He immediately called her woman, signifying he recognised noticeable differences between himself (man) and the woman physically, biologically, and emotionally. Adam's insight was not merely the result of God's impartation or his intuition but his observation. Given that Eve was a grown woman, Adam noticed her attractive breasts, curvy shape, feminine voice, and gentle and caring persona. He was immediately attracted to her and proceeded to compliment her.

"This one is bone from my bone, and flesh from my flesh! She will be called 'woman,' because she was taken from 'man.'"

(Genesis 2:23)

Women are not men's replacements; they uniquely complement them, supporting them in the areas of greatest need. Eve was Adam's solution to the lingering problem, lack of company—God's divine prognosis.

Of all God's creations, man is the only creature personally moulded by God to look like God and rule like God. He is God's product, according to Genesis 1:26.

...and let them have dominion over the fish of the sea, and over the fowl of the air, and over the cattle, and over all the earth, and over every creeping thing that creepeth upon the earth.

(Genesis 1:26)

Given what we know about manufacturers and their products, it is safe to conclude that man was created to fulfil God's purpose within the earth.

Christ is the visible image of the invisible God. He existed before anything was created and is supreme over all creation, for through him God created everything in the heavenly realms and on earth. He made the things we can see and the things we can't see—such as thrones, kingdoms, rulers, and authorities in the unseen world. Everything was created through him and for him. He existed before anything else, and he holds all creation together. ***(Colossians 1:15-18)***

Man is the product of a united and collaborative effort by the Triune God. From scripture above, we can deduce that God is a planning God, and everything He does has an intended outcome. From before the beginning of creation, God had an ultimate plan to design and create people who would worship Him in response to their sincere veneration for Him and serve His purpose within the earth.

Therefore, man is not an afterthought or an element that God decided to put together after he created all of creation; man is carefully designed and made to manage God's resources and the rest of His creation. He is the prime among God's invention created with a superior responsibility. One can insinuate that God perhaps thought, 'now that I have created all of this, I will install him to manage and take care of all that I have made, and man, indeed, became the crowning glory and masterpiece of God's creation.

God first made everything that He desired to be taken care of. Afterward, he created man and installed him to serve immediately, further reinforcing that God prescribed work for man, eliminating any thought of God supporting laziness. Work is not a consequence of s

Affirmations:

- I am God's legal representative in the earth, a visible representation of the invisible God.

- I will maintain a firm and unwavering faith in the God that upholds and sustains me.

- I will endeavour to be in constant communion and communication with God who is my source.

- I promise to honour God in all my ways and be his witness offering prolonged public testimony concerning our relationship.

- I am fully conscious of the roles that I must assume in the family, Church, and Society as a whole.

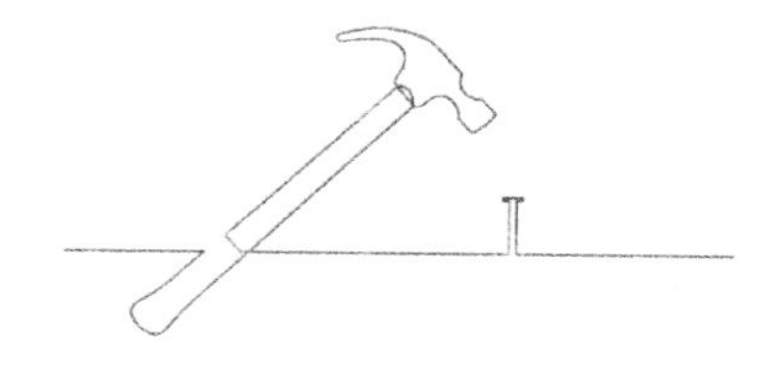

MAN, AND HIS UNIQUENESS AS GOD'S IMAGE

"The image of God carries with it the right not to be mistreated or harmed.... Regardless of their record or character, all human beings have an irreducible glory and significance to them, because God loves them.... So, we must treasure each human being as a way of showing due respect for the majesty of their owner and Creator."

Timothy Keller

Man is not only created in God's image; he is God's image. The word 'image' is coined from the Hebrew word 'tselem', meaning resemblance, something resembling the thing of originality. When designing a new product, it is common for designers to develop a prototype that provides an idea of what the intended outcome will look like and how it will function. God created an identical model that would clearly understand and model His character, nature, and will within the earth. Man was made consistent with God's nature and likeness and had authority to rule within the garden. He acted on God's behalf and had the right to name the creatures and manage the garden. What ever he said was upheld by heaven.

...and let them have dominion over the fish of the sea, and over the fowl of the air, and over the cattle, and over all the earth, and over every creeping thing that creepeth upon the earth.

(Genesis 1:26)

Man commanded the respect of both his colleagues and subordinates alike. To see the man was to see God's representative. He was God's ambassador, capable of making crucial decisions, passing, and enforcing laws within the garden.

And out of the ground the Lord God formed every beast of the field, and every fowl of the air; and brought them unto Adam to see what he would call them: and whatsoever Adam called every living creature that was the name thereof. And Adam gave names to all cattle, and to the fowl of the air, and to every beast of the field; but for Adam there was not found a help meet for him. ***(Genesis 2:19)***

It is pertinent to note that Adam was not God but the image pointing others to God. Though he was not God, he was the closest model on earth to provide a visual concept of God and His nature. He represented God to creation and creation to God. Man is the only creature bearing the likeness of God which helps to explain why incarnation was possible because deity (The real God) and humanity (The prototype) are compatible.

And the Word was made flesh, and dwelt among us, (and we beheld his glory, the glory as of the only begotten of the Father,) full of grace and truth. ***(John 1:14)***

Jesus was a one hundred percent (100%) prototype representing God to man and man to God, and he was also one hundred percent God, the person he was representing.

He was God's representative within the earth to God's creation and the creation's mouthpiece to God. Such understanding will aid man in recognising his purpose within the earth. We can therefore infer man was created to be God's advocate on the earth, ever voicing humanity's concern to their creator. It is a common understanding that if the owner leaves one in charge of his proceeds, he will likely show up unplanned or spontaneous to check on His assets. Man must labour assiduously to fulfil his father's mandate.

"To please our Lord with our work, we recognise that our view of work begins with God Himself. We work because God works, fashioning and upholding this world. He is Creator, King, and Good Shepherd. Our desire to mend what is broken echoes God's resolve to redeem his fallen creation. Our drive to make and fulfil plans follows our Lord, who planned and accomplished redemption. When we embrace a project and rejoice at its completion, we imitate Jesus, who said, "My food is to do the will of him who sent me and to accomplish his work" (John 4:34).

Mankind works because God created us in His image, and He works"- Unknown.

This explains God's frequently scheduled meeting for the cool of the day in the Garden.

And they heard the voice of the Lord God walking in the garden in the cool of the day: and Adam and his wife hid themselves from the presence of the Lord God amongst the trees of the garden. And the Lord God called unto Adam, and said unto him, where art thou? ***(Genesis 3:9)***

Our mandate as His representative is to honour God, always serving His interest as heaven's ambassador to earth providing meaningful feedback to God concerning His work.

Declaration:

Write this declaration and place it somewhere that you visit frequently. Example: Office, car, bathroom.

"I am Unique, and I will live Unique."

Affirmations:

- I commit to co-labour with God for the furtherance of his mission.
- I recognise that I am biologically distinct from the woman but co-equal with her.
- I promise to lead my family to not just read scriptures but obey God.
- I will adopt the model of leadership exemplified by the scriptures in all my interactions with others.

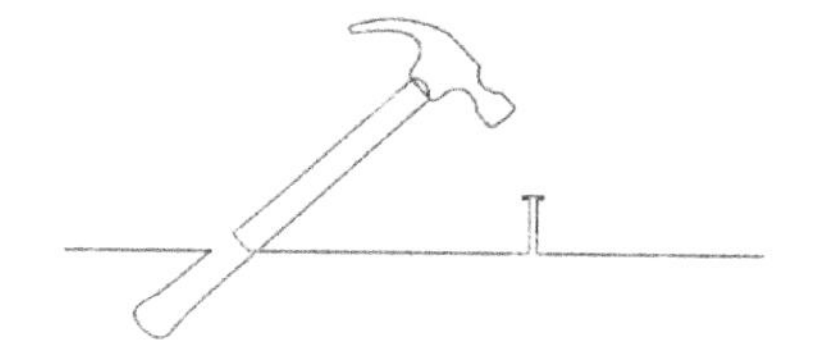

MAN, AND HIS DISTINCTION FROM CREATION

The superior man is the providence of the inferior. He is eyes for the blind, strength for the weak, and a shield for the defenceless. He stands erect by bending above the fallen. He rises by lifting others.

Robert Green Ingersoll

Man was different from all other creations. Noticeably, man was created differently and was set apart from the remaining creation. The Psalmists concur with this idea in his worship to God in the scripture below.

I will praise thee; for I am fearfully and wonderfully made marvellous are thy works; and that my soul knoweth right well.

(Psalms 139:14)

Among God's many creations, man is the only creature created by God to resemble Him. There is a never-ending gap between man and other creations as he is different biologically, morally, intellectually, and spiritually. Below are some of man's features that helps us to understand his uniqueness:

- **Man can speak.** He speaks to both creation and the creator.

- **Man can hear.** He can listen to God, share what he hears, and obey what he is told. He was created to listen to those he leads and represent their needs to God through prayer and supplication.

- **Man has the capacity to respond** with facial and other non-verbal expressions. He has the capacity to converse with man and God beyond speech.

- **Man can make critical decisions** which can either result in him benefiting from a promise or suffering from the consequence of poor decisions.

- **Man possesses personality.** Man is distinct and possesses individuality and uniqueness. Biologically, men are distinct from each other by their very fingerprints.

- **Man has morality.** He is fitted with a moral compass that tells him when he is wrong, even with the absence of laws.

- **Man possesses spirituality.** Man was created to be in fellowship with God and other people consistently. No man is complete by himself, that is, having no need for the support of others. Man is inclined to 'be compassionate and demonstrate mercy to his fellow man. Man possesses a void that can only be satisfied by an intimate relationship with God and a typical relationship with his peers. Man, and God frequently fellowshipped.

When the cool evening breezes were blowing, the man and his wife heard the Lord God walking about in the garden.

(Genesis 3:8)

It would be unusual for the garden owner to refrain from engaging in regular meetings to gain insight into the management and operation of his assets that he has given to man to tend and take care of.

The Lord God placed the man in the Garden of Eden to tend and watch over it. **(Genesis 2:15)**

A meeting implies that God would engage in regular discussions with man, perhaps about himself as steward and other matters relating to the assignment. Frequent correspondence with God was and is still an expectation of God and Jesus to remind man of his obligation to pray.

And he spake a parable unto them to this end, that men ought always to pray, and not to faint. **(Luke 18:1)**

The importance of man conversing with God was reiterated by Paul.

Pray without ceasing. ***(1 Thessalonians 5:17)***

Affirmations:

- I am unique. I am God's workmanship. I possess unique qualities that sets me apart from all of God's creation.

- I am responsible, relatable, empathetic, loving, and hardworking. I will obey God always; His directives are best. I am not a one man's army; I am accountable.

- I will exhibit an unwavering commitment to ensure that all that God has given me to do within the time frame allotted will be accomplished.

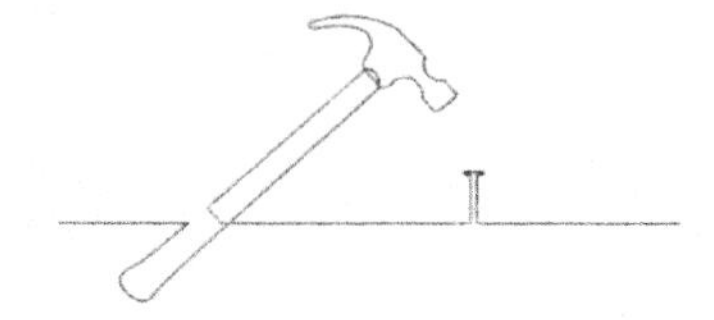

MAN, AND HIS FELLOWSHIP WITH GOD

"A habit of devout fellowship with God is the spring of all our life, and the strength of it."

Henry Edward Manning

Man was created to have fellowship through regular interaction with God. The author of Genesis 3:8 postulates that *"When the cool evening breezes were blowing, the man and his wife heard the Lord God walking about in the garden."*

We can insinuate that God had a close relationship with humanity (Adam and Eve) and thus would often visit them to commune and enjoy a moment of communion with man. Both Adam and Eve expected God to visit; therefore, God was not randomly passing by Eden and deciding to stop; he purposely attended the garden to have fellowship. The word fellowship, coined from the Greek word 'koinonia,' means association, community, communion, and joint participation. Therefore, God intended a relationship characterised by mutual interest embodying frequent sharing, and common bonding, in which both parties share a common goal. It means Adam and Eve wants what God wants. Can you imagine a perfect relationship established on obedience and submission to God's will because you wholeheartedly care about his glory?

This was all God desired from Adam, which is still His preference today. Honour Him through obedience and live in total submission to the eternal God.

And the Lord God commanded the man, saying, of every tree of the garden thou mayest freely eat: But of the tree of the knowledge of good and evil, thou shalt not eat of it: for in the day that thou eatest thereof thou shalt surely die.

(Genesis 2:16-17)

The seemingly evil thing within the text was not the tree but rather the 'act.' It was disobedience that distorted the relationship between God and man. Man's choice went against God's recommendation and caused him to transgress, violating a laid down principle. Therefore, continued fellowship correlates to our sincere and purposeful obedience to God.

If ye love me, keep my commandments. ***(John 14:15)***

Obedience derives from love and a passion to honour. Fellowship grounded in obedience, love, and submission is lasting, fulfilling, and satisfying. There is no record of irregularities predating man's disobedience.

Fellowship also implies a common interest between God and man: God cares about the man and his concerns, and man, in turn, cares about God. This is the sole rationale for obedience; the man was to demonstrate his love through 'hearing hearts.' The idea of hearing hearts is generated from the Hebrew phrase 'shema levot' and means to live in obedience to God because of your unconditional love for Him and His ways. Peter expresses an accurate understanding of such fellowship:

Give all your worries and cares to God, for he cares about you.

(1 Peter 5:7)

The resounding reality is that man is made to commune and communicate with God on matters of mutual interest. Communion suggests that both parties (man and God) are interdependent and interrelated, share the same resources, and are bound by the same responsibilities. As the prototype, man is committed to creation as God does. You may be wondering, isn't God fully functional without man? Yes, He is, but He desires to partner with man.

Though man is God's prototype (made in the image of God), God does not have a physical or human body. Jesus explains that God is a Spirit.

For God is Spirit, so those who worship him must worship in spirit and in truth. **(John 4:24)**

Think of man as a flowchart consisting of diagrams and arrows showing how data flow within a program. The illustrations help you to comprehend the nature and functionality of the program. The program has no physical shapes or graphical illustrations and cannot be seen. However, it works and functions exactly as illustrated in the model. Therefore, whereas God does not possess a physical body, he has created man as a flowchart that showcases what God sees, hears, touches, speaks, thinks, plans, develops, leads, rules, loves, commends, and teaches.

Affirmations:

- I am confident that the work that God has started in me will be completed.

- I will not rest until my life's mission of ensuring that other men begin to recognise their identity in Christ comes to fruition.

- I will both listen to God and commit to action what he has said.

- I understand that prayer is never complete until God answers.

- I will patiently endure until I receive God's promises.

- I will not be distracted by any other voices that disagree with the premise of God's word.

- I will use my faith to dispel my fears.

- I will influence the lives of others even as I am influenced in my life by God.

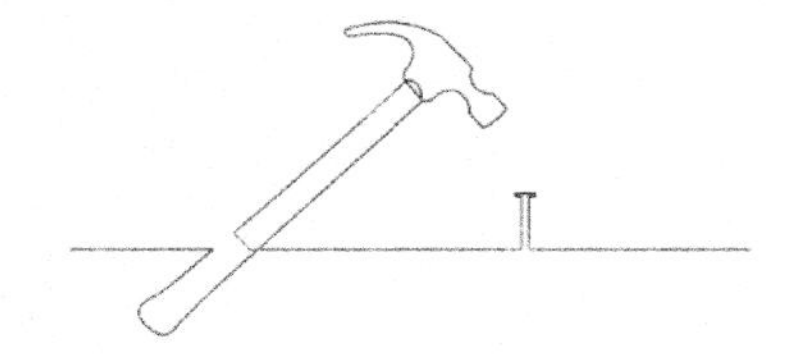

MAN, AND HIS GODLY LIKENESS

The superior man honours his virtuous nature, and maintains constant inquiry and study, seeking to carry it out to its breadth and greatness, to omit none of the more exquisite and minute points which it embraces, and to raise it to its greatest height and brilliancy.

Confucius

Man was made into God's Likeness. Image and likeness often carry the same meaning; however, within this context, we would like to distinguish between the terms. The word 'image' suggests that man physically represents God. That is, man having an ear, implies that God hears, a mouth suggests He speaks, eyes are evidence He sees, feet show He moves, and hands indicate He does. The image of God (Latin, imago dei) refers to the immaterial part of humanity. It sets human beings apart from the animal world, fits them for the dominion God intended them to have over the earth. This uniquely enables them to commune with their Maker.

Then God blessed them and said, "Be fruitful and multiply. Fill the earth and govern it. Reign over the fish in the sea, the birds in the sky, and all the animals that scurry along the ground."

(Genesis 1:28)

Man's uniqueness transcends physical appearance. He distinguishes himself mentally, socially, and morally.

Man is created as a rational, volitional agent to reason and choose which reflects God's intellect, freedom, and power. Whenever man invents a machine, writes a book, discover a vaccine, paints a landscape, enjoys a symphony, calculates a sum, or names a pet, he is proclaiming that he is made in God's image, having the ability to recognise a problem, critically analyse, and generate a workable solution. Consequently, we are made in His image mentally and intellectually.

Furthermore, man possesses social tendencies borne from his maker. He was created for fellowship reflecting God's triune nature and His love. In Eden, man's primary relationship was with God.

When the cool evening breezes were blowing, the man[a] and his wife heard the LORD God walking about in the garden. So, they hid from the LORD God among the trees. ***(Genesis 3:8)***

Man is relational; he is built to interact with his maker and fellow man. God later made the first woman because "it is not good for the man to be alone".

Then the LORD God said, "It is not good for the man to be alone. I will make a helper who is just right for him." ***(Genesis 2:18)***

Whenever man marries, makes a friend, hugs a child, or attends church, he is demonstrating that he is made in the image of God.

Finally, man is a moral being representing his maker. He was created in righteousness having perfect innocence, reflecting God's absolute holiness.

God saw all He had made (humanity included) and called it "very good". ***(Genesis 1:31)***

Our conscience or "moral compass" is a vestige of that original state. Whenever man writes a law, voice opposition to terror and oppression, defends the poor, rejects hostility, recoils from evil, praises good behaviour, or feels guilty, he is affirming that he is made in God's image.

On the other hand, likeness implies that man possesses the qualities of God, including:

- **He has authority.** Historically, it was common practice among the heathen nations for kings to set up images to show forth their rule and authority and even demand worship. The image represented the king's rule and authority within that kingdom. An example is observed in Daniel 3: 1-3:

King Nebuchadnezzar made a gold statue ninety feet tall and nine feet wide and set it up on the plain of Dura in the province of Babylon. Then he sent messages to the high officers, officials, governors, advisers, treasurers, judges, magistrates, and all the provincial officials to come to the dedication of the statue he had set up. So, all these officials came and stood before the statue King Nebuchadnezzar had set up. ***(Daniel 3:1-3)***

Man's physical presence on earth indicates and represents God's rule and authority within the earth. Unlike other heathen images that received praise for themselves, he is expected to worship God and direct others to serve Him. To see the man is to see the 'King of king of 'kings' holy, sovereign, and mighty. God authorises man to rule and have dominion over all things living and non-living within the earth. Man gives and directs praise to God.

They will reign over the fish in the sea, the birds in the sky, the livestock, all the wild animals on the earth, and the small animals that scurry along the ground. ***(Genesis 1:26)***

Man was designed superior with the ability to affect changes within the earth, and God gave him dominion to reign. Dominion is translated from the Hebrew word 'radah', which means to rule, dominate, subjugate, prevail against, and tread down. It is within the man's DNA to lead, modify, alter, improve upon, and make better. He should lead his family to God and preside over his household with wisdom.

- **He is compassionate.** Man draws his identity from God. One of God's attributes is that he is solicitous, tender-hearted, empathetic, and sympathetic.

As a father pities his children, so the LORD pities those who fear Him. ***(Psalms 103:13)***

In the text cited above, David described God's love as comparable to the endless and underserving love that good earthly fathers possess and display for their children despite their frailties and weaknesses. Perhaps the writer wanted to highlight that a good father only wants what is best for his children, and even in cases requiring discipline, the love remains intact. Despite Adam's sin, God's love for him remained. Although he was banished from the garden, God continued to support and care for him. The presence of discipline does not mean the absence of love. Soon after his termination from the garden, his older son Cain killed his younger son Abel. While holding Cain accountable, he was expected to show the same measure of concern, warmth, and consideration towards his son, Cain. As God's prototype, he was not at liberty to hate or ill-treat his son despite his blatant sin. Today men are expected to show kindness and understanding towards their children and should desist from provoking them.

And ye fathers, provoke not your children to wrath: but bring them up in the nurture and admonition of the Lord.

(Ephesians 6:4)

- **He is relatable.** Adam, being in charge, meant that he would need to interact with Eve concerning matters of stewardship and, therefore, would need to be approachable, friendly, helpful, and supportive. These are all qualities possessed by God.

Let us therefore come boldly unto the throne of grace that we may obtain mercy and find grace to help in time of need.

(Hebrews 4:16)

- **He reconciles.** Man should confess his faults, apologise for his mistakes, show compassion to others, and forgive those who have offended him.

Make allowance for each other's faults and forgive anyone who offends you. Remember, the Lord forgave you, so you must forgive others. **(Colossians 3:13)**

God is man's great example. He is the eternal restorer of man. Since he made the product, he can repair it. Scripture shows God's willingness to restore man to his original and perfect state.

Arise, and go down to the potter's house, and there I will cause thee to hear my words. Then I went down to the potter's house, and behold, he wrought a work on the wheels. And the vessel that he made of clay was marred in the hand of the potter: so, he made it again another vessel, as seemed good to the potter to make it. ***(Jerimiah 18:2-4)***

- **He is responsible.** The immutable God presented Himself to Adam in the garden as a judge holding him accountable and as a restorer to reinstate him into fellowship.

And the Lord God called unto Adam, and said unto him, where art thou? And he said, I heard thy voice in the garden, and I was afraid, because I was naked; and I hid myself. And he said, who told thee that thou wast naked? Hast, thou eaten of the tree, whereof I commanded thee that thou shouldest not eat? And the man said, the woman whom thou gavest to be with me, she gave me of the tree, and I did eat. **(Genesis 3:8-12)**

Man's inability to accept responsibility for his error and failure to recognise the need for restoration affected the outcome. Given what we know about God and His unabating love, compassion, and willingness to restore, Adam's response to God could have influenced the outcome. Whereas the act was punished, the never-ending love of God remained intact.

And unto Adam he said, Because thou hast hearkened unto the voice of thy wife, and hast eaten of the tree, of which I commanded thee, saying, Thou shalt not eat of it: cursed is the ground for thy sake; in sorrow shalt thou eat of it all the days of thy life; Thorns also and thistles shall it bring forth to thee; and thou shalt eat the herb of the field; In the sweat of thy face shalt thou eat bread, till thou return unto the ground; for out of it was thou taken: for dust thou art, and unto dust shalt thou return. ***(Genesis 3:17)***

Despite interrogating Adam first, he was the last to be sanctioned. It was almost like God was saying, 'you were created to serve and to dominate; not only did you fail in this act of disobedience, but you blundered in your role as steward.' This trait is pictured in Galatians 6:1, where Paul explains that an underlying spiritual characteristic must be the willingness to restore another who has erred.

Brethren, if a man be overtaken in a fault, ye which are spiritual, restore such a one in the spirit of meekness; considering thyself, lest thou also be tempted.

(Galatians 6:1)

- **He is loving.** Man must show love towards his fellowman irrespective of difference in opinions. He must epitomise the love of His maker God who possesses an undying love for humanity.

For God so loved the world, that he gave his only begotten Son, that whosoever believeth in him should not perish, but have everlasting life. **(John 3: 16)**

Irrespective of the fall of man, God's love was unchanged. Man, God's image within the earth, must epitomise this type of love.

Be devoted to one another in love. Honour one another above yourselves. **(Romans 12:10)**

- **He nourishes.** The term nourish means to cause to grow or live in a healthy state, especially by providing good nutrients. As we examine the text in Genesis 2, we see God positioning Himself as the ultimate provider, sustainer, and keeper of man.

And the Lord God planted a garden eastward in Eden; and there he put the man whom he had formed. And out of the ground made the Lord God to grow every tree that is pleasant to the sight, and good for food, the tree of life also in the midst of the garden, and the tree of knowledge of good and evil. **(Genesis 2:8-9)**

And the Lord God commanded the man, saying, Of every tree of the garden thou mayest freely eat: **Genesis 2:16)**

Paul confidently admonished the Philippian church that God would continuously care for their needs.

And my God shall supply all your needs according to His riches in glory by Christ Jesus. **(Philippians 4:19)**

In the same way, God provides for His people; the man should provide for his family.

But if any provide not for his own, and especially for those of his own house, he hath denied the faith, and is worse than an infidel. **(1 Timothy 5:8)**

- **He cares.** Scripture teaches that God is caring towards his people.

Humble yourselves therefore under the mighty hand of God, that he may exalt you in due time: Casting all your care upon him; for he careth for you. **(1 Peter 5:6-7)**

Comparatively, man should demonstrate care towards his household.

Wives, submit yourselves unto your own husbands, as it is fit in the Lord. **(Colossians 3:18)**

"In the social jungle of human existence, there is no feeling of being alive without a sense of identity."-Erik Erikson

Reflection:

- What are qualities I naturally demonstrate?
- What are those areas that I need improvement?

Affirmations:

- I will represent God morally, socially, and mentally.
- I am God's ambassador in the earth bearing all His qualities.
- I am like God in that I do what God does. My thoughts are in sync with God's plans.
- My actions confirm I am His representative.
- I will lay a proper financial foundation from my family.
- I will ensure that money is always my servant and never my master.

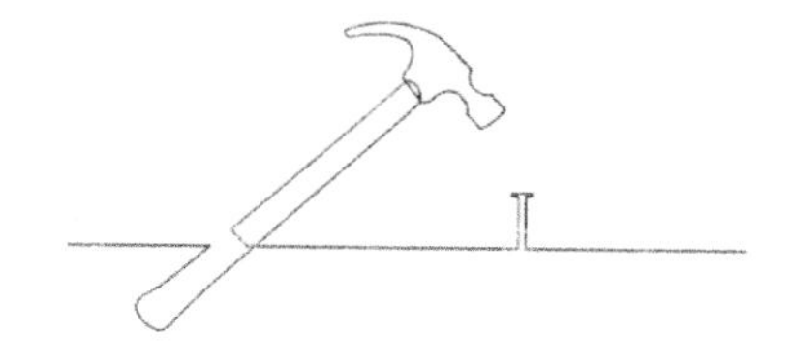

MAN, AND HIS PRESCRIBED INDIVIDUALITY

"To be yourself in a world that is constantly trying to make you something else is the greatest accomplishment."

Ralph Waldo Emerson

The man's individuality is defined by his creator and not by society. Views within our contemporary world change quite quickly and vary among cultures; therefore, identity founded on such grounds is likely to lead to an identity crisis breathed from confusion. Man preceded and predated culture and the intent for his design and role he would play can only be retrieved from God. Only God knows the reason he made man and the role he would play within His mission. The book of Genesis provided a comprehensive framework for man to discover his identity as defined by God. This framework highlights the ensuing truths:

- Man was created to be God's image within the earth, demonstrating Godly traits in his stewardship and among his fellow man.

- He is designed to reflect God's attributes within the earth, such as showing kindness, care, support, and help towards each other.

- Man is the authorised and legitimate leader responsible for showcasing God to family and likewise advocates for them through prayer.

- Man is superior to animals having features that suggest that he sees, hears, comprehends, feels, and speaks.

- Man is created to serve God's will.

- Man is responsible, loving, understanding, caring, relatable, and industrious.

- Man is worthwhile and is the fruit of a meticulous plan by God.

- Man is meant to be perfect in obedience to God and His word.

- Man is accountable to himself, his family, fellowman, and God.

- Man is complete and approved by God as being fearfully and wonderfully made.

- He is disciplined and serves his role with distinction.

- He is faithful and committed to God's mission.

- He bears Godly characteristics and is often described as Godly or Christ-like.

- Man is a male and is biologically, intellectually, and socially proven.

- Man is a good communicator who frequently dialogues with his mates and speaks to God through prayer.

Peter sums up the man's identity as being kingly in his declaration:

But ye are a chosen generation, a royal priesthood, a holy nation, a peculiar people; that ye should shew forth the praises of him who hath called you out of darkness into his marvellous light.

(1 Peter 2:9)

Jesus describes the man as a friend:

Henceforth I call you not servants; for the servant knoweth not what his lord doeth: but I have called you friends; for all things that I have heard of my Father I have made known unto you.

(John 15:15)

Paul described the man as God's handiwork.

For we are his workmanship, created in Christ Jesus unto good works, which God hath before ordained that we should walk in them.

Affirmations:

- I am who God says I am.
- I am created for His purpose. I am good communicator who frequently speaks to God through prayer.
- I am fearfully and wonderfully made; your works are wonderful; I know that full well.

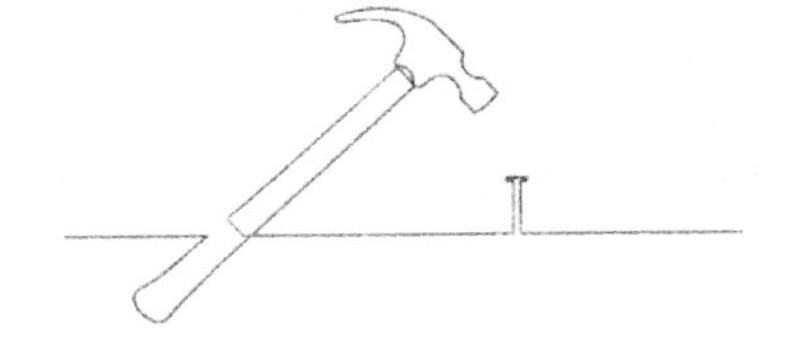

MAN, AND HIS CALL TO REFUTE DELUSIONS

The superior man honours his virtuous nature, and maintains constant inquiry and study, seeking to carry it out to its breadth and greatness, to omit none of the more exquisite and minute points which it embraces, and to raise it to its greatest height and brilliancy.

Confucius

Psychology argues that identity has to do with a self-image, that is, one's mental model self. However, this is inconsistent with Biblical orthodoxy. There is no comprehension of identity outside of the creator, and man cannot know his worth, void of the knowledge of his maker. He was created to be God's image, and he embodies his creators' qualities and models His conduct.

Just as we have borne the image of the man of dust, we shall also bear the image of the man of heaven. ***(1Corinthians 15:49)***

Peter Weinreich opines, "A man's identity is the totality of his self-construal." He further argues that "how man construes himself in the present expresses the continuity between how he sees himself in the past and the future, referred to as ethnic identity. However, man's identity is not solely hinged on his understanding of the past and aspirations for the future but on his knowledge of God and what God's Word states regarding man and his purpose. God first labelled man, suggesting He knew who He was making and the purpose He would serve on the earth. Man can better understand identity by comprehending God's intent for making him as defined in His word. Only God can clarify identity. He affirms our identity through continuous fellowship.

Wenreich further breaks down identity into a subcategory called gender identity. This is the degree to which one views oneself as a person and concerning other people, ideas, and nature. This is incomplete when compared to God's word. The Bible clearly teaches that God is the definer of gender.

So, God created man in his own image, in the image of God created he him; male and female created he them. **(Genesis 1:27)**

Affirmations:

- I affirm that I am a man and that my identity is with Christ in God.

- I was designed and created by God to fulfil his purpose within the earth.

- I have been endowed with both capabilities and capacities to function in the areas of my assignment.

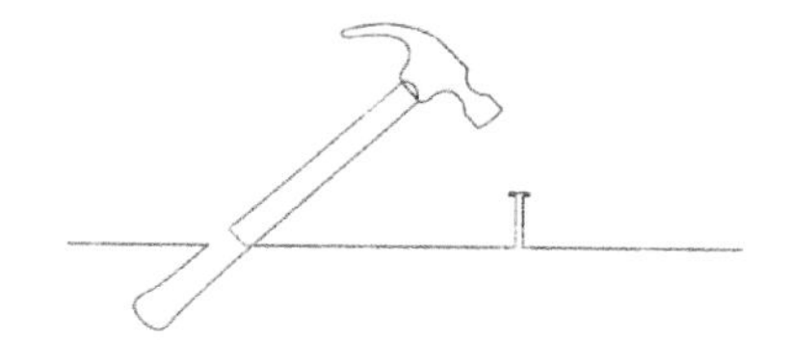

MAN, AND HIS CREATOR

The more I study nature, the more I stand amazed at the work of the Creator. Science brings men nearer to God.
Louis Pasteur

Defining man requires us to examine the relationship he shares with His God. First, we must establish that he was created to share fellowship with God.

So, we are lying if we say we have fellowship with God but go on living in spiritual darkness; we are not practicing the truth. But if we are living in the light, as God is in the light, then we have fellowship with each other, and the blood of Jesus, his Son, cleanses us from all sin. ***(1 John 1:6)***

The term 'fellowship' originates from the Greek word 'Koinonia', meaning partnership. There is an inextricable link between God and man; he is wired to God and cannot exist outside of God.

For in him we live, and move, and have our being; as certain also of your own poets have said, for we are also his offspring.

(Acts 17:28)

The fact that man was personally fashioned, moulded, and formed by God implies the degree to which God regards man as being set apart from all His other creations.

And the Lord God formed man of the dust of the ground...

(Genesis 1:7a)

'Dust' figuratively represents something of little worth. God used the very basic element of the earth to create a being who would forever reflect on the goodness of God and, in humility, submits to Him and His authority. An awareness of the material from which he was constructed should inspire him to live in meekness while expressing gratitude to God. The idea of being created from dust reiterates that man cannot exist without God; perhaps this consciousness motivated Abraham's modest response to God in Genesis 18:

Then Abraham answered and said, *"Indeed now, I who am but dust and ashes have taken it upon myself to speak to the Lord:* ***(Genesis 18:27)***

Abraham's address highlights the posture of a reflective man who, when measuring himself to the sovereign God, adopts a position of humility. Conceivably Abraham reasoned, "this God existed independent of man, formed him out of the very element I presently stand on. I cannot demand anything; rather, I must beg everything. This attitude epitomises effective prayer derived from intentional and deliberate submission to God. Our knowledge of God should reveal understanding of our identity, which is inadequate and insufficient without God. As unique as we are, we are the only by-product (made from another product) in creation. God wanted man, irrespective of his accomplishment as a leader on the earth, to regularly introspect, recalling that he is just dust. John belaboured this when he declared that man would not have existed without God.

In the beginning was the Word, and the Word was with God, and the Word was God. The same was in the beginning with God. All things were made by him; and without him was not anything made that was mad. **(John 1:1-3)**

Man without God is nothing. On the contrary, God without man is still God. We are fully dependent on our self-existing, self-reliable, and self-dependent God.

After forming man from the earth's dust, God blew His breath into man's nostrils.

...and breathed into his nostrils the breath of life; and man became a living soul. **(Genesis 2:7)**

Interestingly it was not the beautiful shell created by God that accounted for the life man possessed but the breath God deposited into his nostrils. The man laid lifeless, helpless, and useless even after his construction was completed. This explains the degree to which we are reliant on God. The divine breath transformed a stiff, fruitless, and bootless shell into a living being, giving him purpose and mandate to tend and care for his assignment. Identity and purpose are wrapped up solely in the product's guide, God's word.

The man was created to bring pleasure to God. The ultimate purpose for man and the remainder of God's creation was to bring pleasure to God.

The word 'pleasure' originates from the Greek word 'aresko', meaning pleasing and acceptable. Throughout Genesis 1, we see God reporting after every creation that it was good. 'Good' in this text is extracted from the Hebrew word 'tob', meaning possessing desirable qualities, pleasant, valuable, and beneficial. God's reflection on His creation gave Him a sense of happiness, joy, and delight as He carefully observed His handiwork. Unequivocally man was created for one core reason: to bring pleasure to God. We please God when we obey His commands and worship Him out of an abundance of joy. John recorded an account in Revelation in which the four hundred and twenty elders bowed and worshiped God saying:

Thou art worthy, O Lord, to receive glory and honour and power: for thou hast created all things, and for thy pleasure they are and were created. ***(Revelation 4:11)***

Man as a creation of God is distinct in destiny and purpose. You cannot know the product without consulting the manufacturer. Similarly, man cannot know His purpose and value without engaging in fruitful communication with God, his maker. Previously, the writers explained that one of the fundamental truths about man is that he was made in the image and likeness of God. As with Adam, the first man, contemporary males are expected to live in a way that resembles God. They must show forth the virtues of God by and through their lifestyle, submit to the Holy Spirit, and pattern their life after the Word of God.

Jesus taught His believers the ensuing qualities:

- *Blessed are the poor in spirit: for theirs is the kingdom of heaven.*
- *Blessed are they that mourn for they shall be comforted.*
- *Blessed are the meek: for they shall inherit the earth.*
- *Blessed are they which do hunger and thirst after righteousness: for they shall be filled.*
- *Blessed are the merciful: for they shall obtain mercy.*
- *Blessed are the pure in heart: for they shall see God.*

- *Blessed are the peacemakers: for they shall be called the children of God.*

- *Blessed are they which are persecuted for righteousness' sake: for theirs is the kingdom of heaven.*

- *Blessed are ye, when men shall revile you, and persecute you, and shall say all manner of evil against you falsely, for my sake.* **(Matthew 5:2-11)**

Man's likeness to God distinguishes him from the rest of God's creation. Man is a personal being with the power to think, feel, and decide, and he can make moral choices and he has the capacity for spiritual growth or decline. In the beginning, the man loved God and was a holy being.

Paul reiterates the need for believers, particularly men to possess these characteristics in his address to the Galatians.

But the fruit of the Spirit is love, joy, peace, longsuffering, gentleness, goodness, faith, Meekness, temperance.

(Galatians 5: 22-23)

A man, therefore, possesses the qualities of the creator; therefore, His actions and conduct should be parallel to the nature of God. We can therefore infer that manliness is directly correlated (synonymous) to Godliness. The closer his relationship to his creator, the more he reflects God and the more confident he will become. This helps to explain the need for constant prayer. Prayer is the avenue through which man relates to God and becomes aware of God's expectations. The more man prays, the more he reflects his creator and ultimately learns to mirror God's standards.

"You are born a male, but you become a man. You cannot become what you don't know."- Edwin Cole

The Biblical account of the Garden of Eden shows that the deceiver deceived man into dishonouring God. This decision was devastating and fractured the man's identity, causing him to lose sight of his purpose. Man became a trespasser of God's law, and his action had severe consequences; it did not only affect him but his offspring.

When Adam sinned, sin entered the world. Adam's sin brought death, so death spread to everyone, for everyone sinned.

(Romans 5:12)

To represent God on the earth, man needed to be restored. Man's absence from the relationship did not mean expulsion from God's love. His error did not equate to sustained rejection and condemnation but led to God's perfect reconciliation plan. God hated the act of sin (transgression against His laws). Whereas the consequence for the unfortunate action excluded him from the physical place of residence, God's love for man remained intact, unchanged, and continuous. Like Adam, we have erred against God's Biblical standards; however, we can be assured that God loves His image, man.

"For this is how God loved the world: He gave his one and only Son, so that everyone who believes in him will not perish but have eternal life. **(John 3:16)**

The loving, compassionate, and caring God offered the ultimate sacrifice as an invaluable gift in His bid to redeem man. If God was this willing to pursue man's redemption, be cognisant that you are special, loved, and valuable. Yes, you! It does not matter your socio-economic status, race, language, nationality, ethnicity, or level of intelligence; God loves you and has invested in your redemption.

Therefore, if any man be in Christ, he is a new creature: old things are passed away; behold, all things are become new.

Man sharing a bond with God does not merely result in a modified version of himself but a new creature. This implies that a man in fellowship with Christ is not a repaired or refurbished individual; instead, he is regenerated to represent the KING again.

Clarke as cited in Guzik (2018) postulates that *"The man is not only mended, but he is new made… there is a new creation, which God himself owns as his workmanship, and which he can look on and pronounce very good."*

Reflection:

Use five words to describe your creator.

Affirmations:

- I am fully yielded to the Holy Spirit so the very life and virtues of Christ shall be manifested through my life and witness.

- I affirm that my relationship with Christ is the most important aspect of my life.

- I declare that nothing will separate me from the love of God that is in Christ Jesus.

- I will continue to be God's standard bearer and influencer on the earth.

- I am cognizant that I am the creation of God and his steward in the earth.

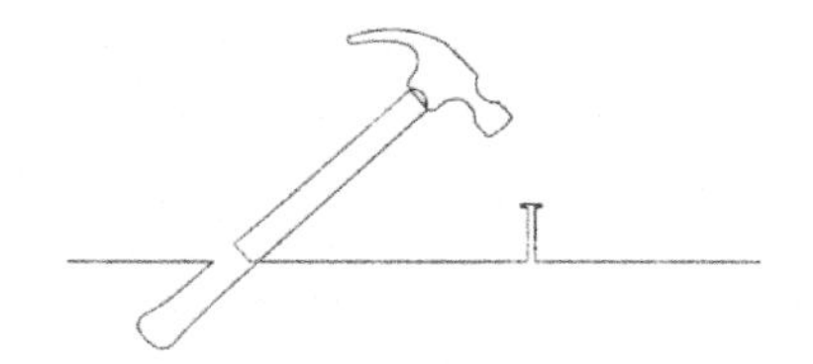

MAN, AND ULTIMATE VISION FOR HIM

"Draw near to God, and he will draw near to you.".

(James 4:8)

Throughout history God has enacted varying systems of restoration and raised up deliverers as a sign of His unwavering love for man.

For the sin of this one man, Adam, caused death to rule over many. But even greater is God's wonderful grace and his gift of righteousness, for all who receive it will live in triumph over sin and death through this one man, Jesus Christ.

(Romans 5:17)

The first man was made and not born; therefore, he was made entirely, having no need to grow and develop physically. All his knowledge was derived from God, and his experience was drawn from his interaction with his surroundings. He was the epitome of God's perfect and complete work made in God's image and likeness, and he ruled the earth with distinction. This sets out the standard for man today. He must grow, develop into God's image and likeness, and lead, administer, guide, support his family, and undertake any other assigned tasks. Man, today can only maximise his true worth when he embodies an interrelation with his God. Man outside of a covenantal relationship with God is incomplete; all other males are developed, processed, and socialised into becoming a man. A thorough understanding of God's word to man and consistent praying are crucial to the development of man. Since God is the creator, He possesses the details regarding man's purpose and value. Therefore, the search for purpose and worth begins with pursuing fellowship with God.

A man gets his identity from his responsibilities as specified by his maker. There is an inextricable link between man and what he is expected to do and accomplish. Man's formation was in keeping with the role that God expected him to fulfil. He was wired to work and integrate himself into all aspects of the earth, fulfilling the requirements of God. He represented that link between a sovereign God and the created order. A man is therefore identified not only by who he is but also by what he does. He has been placed upon the earth to represent God in all he does. What he does is a visible representation of who God is. Man's involvement in work predates the fall. Thus, the man acting responsibly is not a consequence of sin but him fulfilling his purpose.

The second Adam (Jesus) opines, "if you see me, you have seen the father." Jesus is the prototype, but He is not the Father. To see the prototype is to gain insight into the actual entity. The presence of man is always indicative of the reality of God, and creation can't exist without a creator.

Affirmations:

- I am conscious that having been born a male I must become a man.
- I fully recognise and endorse that manliness and Godliness are synonymous.
- I promise to be faithful in maintaining an unbroken communication and fellowship with God.
- I am thankful that I am the workmanship of God called and created to represent him by good works.
- I promise to listen to God twice as much as I speak with him.

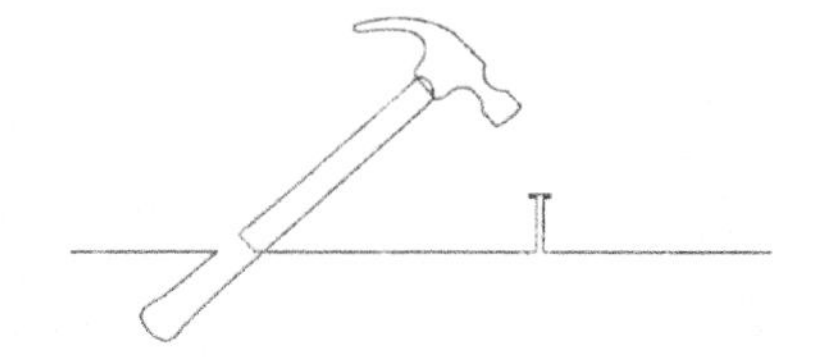

MAN, AND HIS PURPOSE

"Your purpose in life is to find your purpose and give your whole heart and soul to it."

Unknown

At some point in life, we must all interface with the ensuing questions:

- What is my purpose?
- Do I have a purpose?
- How do I know my purpose?

Purpose seeks to explain why we are here. It is the reason for existence. As with everything else created, man was created to serve the purpose intended by God. Every product is designed to solve a problem or resolve a pending situation. Let us examine a chair's purpose for instance. The chair was not created and later assigned its role, but rather it was designed with the role in mind; it was made to be solution in response to a need of people; to sit. In like manner, the Apostolic Writings explain that in the beginning, God created the Heavens and the Earth. Given what we know about purpose, we can assume that God made the heavens and the earth for His glory. Such careful construction with a personal touch means it is valuable and meaningful to God. Using our earthly experience, we could infer that if God took the time to call forth creation into existence, He perhaps thought that the "eternal void" would be more attractive and complete with these inventions. Having constructed the earth, He created, installed, and appointed man as the steward to tend and care for the planet.

To better understand man's purpose, there is a need to consult with the creator's manual.

The Lord God placed the man in the Garden of Eden to tend and watch over it. **(Genesis 2:15)**

Therefore, caring for the earth is a core part of man's purpose. Today, with the advancement of technology, machinery, and other development, we are experiencing long-term changes in the average weather patterns, better known as climate change. Research in recent times has suggested that the earth is being affected by global warming (human-induced warming of the earth's system). The continuous mining of the earth's surface to produce iron needed to create machinery and infrastructure has also impacted the globe. Similarly, burning fossil fuels has also contributed to many of the changes we are now experiencing. Over the years, varying governments and interest groups have enacted and enforced rules locally and internationally to preserve the earth. However, much more needs to be done. Men are strategically positioned within various sectors of society to influence change and encourage support for laws and practices that will protect the earth.

Some steps that we can take to preserve the earth are:

Speak Up and Speak Out: We have greater access to information. Likewise, we have various platforms; therefore, we must use them to encourage people to find methods and mechanisms that are less harmful to the earth. The protection of the planet is not limited to government and environmental groups, but it is one of the fundamental roles of all men.

Model the expected behaviour: Often we are responsible for littering. Other times we turn a blind eye to those who litter. Such acts are irresponsible and only contributes to the year-old problem of pollution. What can we do? We can become advocates for change, modelling the expected behaviour and inspiring others to do the same. We must research and adopt the appropriate steps to reduce littering or any action that could negatively impact the earth. These include recycling instead of burning, eating sustainably, and using less petrol. Research shows that what we eat contributes to at least a quarter of greenhouse gases worldwide.

We must collectively work to preserve the earth through education and personal actions. We must exemplify this in our homes, workspaces, and worship centres. Doing so will socialise our children and prepare them to be tomorrow's stewards. God has endowed man with the ability to formulate, develop and implement best practices that would auger well for sustainability.

Direct your children onto the right path, and when they are older, they will not leave it. **(Proverbs 22:6)**

Man's purpose also includes administering and leading over God's affairs and representing God on Earth. The man was created and wired with attributes to lead and manage. The first man acquired the skills and expertise necessary to serve from the most reliable source; God. Today, God uses various mediums, such as schools to aid us with the requisite skills to excel in leadership and administration. Leadership is more than a post or position to which we are appointed but more so the roles those offices require us to fulfil. It must include how the man perceives himself. We are who God says we are, whether serving in an earthly office or not. It is not the appointment that makes us leaders but God Himself. The word of God, coupled with our application, will aid us in becoming leaders. Appointed or not by a person or entity, God has created us to "lead." In whatever capacity we serve, we do so as leaders. We are to exhibit these qualities regardless of society's definition.

...Reign over the fish in the sea, the birds in the sky, and all the animals that scurry along the ground. ***(Genesis 1:28b)***

To read more on man's purpose as a leader consider getting our book: Winning at Leading: A Critical Guide to Effective Leadership and Administration.

Man's purpose also involves procreation.

Then God blessed them and said, "Be fruitful and multiply. Fill the earth and govern it. ***(Genesis 1:28a)***

Childbearing and rearing are the media through which humans continue to exist, so God was intentional when he did not only encourage sexual pleasure but reproduction. By doing this responsibly, the man is fulfilling the role that only a man can do despite the ongoing advent of Science and Research, which is one of the reasons why the authors of this book reject any lifestyle that contradicts or undermines this command in scripture.

Then God blessed them and said, "Be fruitful and multiply. Fill the earth and govern it. Reign over the fish in the sea, the birds in the sky, and all the animals that scurry along the ground."

(Genesis 1:28)

Throughout history, various groups have supported same-sex relations, abortions, and other feminist agenda that discourages childbearing; however, we hold fast to the instructions in the scriptures. Paul admonished Timothy:

<u>All Scripture is inspired by God</u> and is useful to teach us what is true and to make us realise what is wrong in our lives. It corrects us when we are wrong and teaches us to do what is right. God uses it to prepare and equip his people to do every good work. ***(2 Timothy 3:16-17)***

Throughout Jesus' ministry, he warned against the antichrist and its agenda. The antichrist is anything that opposes, seeks to replace, or encourages one to ignore God, His word, and His will. Any practice that seeks to eliminate or disregard procreation as a part of man's role is erroneous and should be discouraged. This act of procreation should be exercised within a covenantal relationship between the man and his wife, as supported by the scriptures.

"Therefore, shall a man leave his father and his mother and shall cleave unto his wife: and they shall be one flesh."

(Genesis 2:24)

And he answered and said unto them, have ye not read, that he which made them at the beginning made them male and female, and said, for this cause shall a man leave father and mother, and shall cleave to his wife: and they twain shall be one flesh? Wherefore they are no more twain, but one flesh. What therefore God hath joined together, let not man put asunder.

(Matthew 19:4-6)

The Bible makes it abundantly clear that God created man and that He created him for His glory. Therefore, the ultimate purpose of man, according to the Bible, is simply to glorify God. We fulfil our purpose of glorifying God also by living our lives in relationship and faithful service to Him. Jesus, who was fully man, opines:

I brought glory to you here on earth by completing the work you gave me to do. ***(John 17:4)***

Whatever we do must ultimately bring God glory. Use every opportunity to serve God's interest.

So whether you eat or drink, or whatever you do, do it all for the glory of God. ***(1 Corinthians 10:31)***

Reflection:

Think about all the ways you have impacted people throughout your life. Then declare I am purposeful.

Affirmations:

- I affirm that I know who I am and why I am on the earth.
- I am a unique creation of God and wired for success.
- I will promote God's interest in every sphere of my undertakings.
- I recognise that as a leader I am always accountable to God who will ultimately evaluate my stewardship.

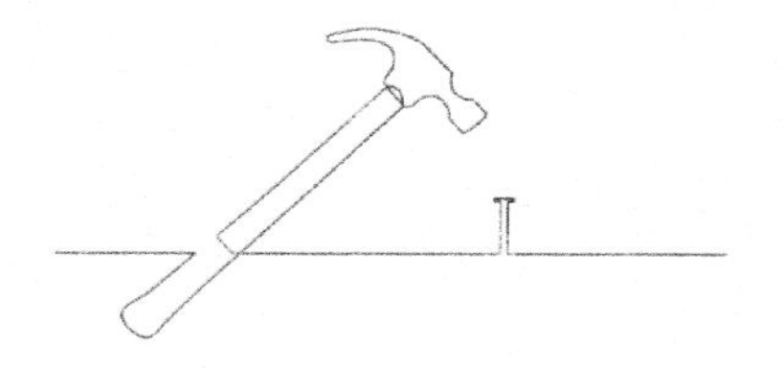

MAN, AND HIS CHILDREN

"The nature of impending fatherhood is that you are doing something that you're unqualified to do, and then you become qualified while doing it."

John Green

Man's highest call is to epitomise God's nature when it comes to his relationship to others more specifically his children. The Bible is clear that all people are God's creation (Colossians 1:16) and that God loves the entire world, good or bad (John 15:13), and desires to restore them (John 3:16). Like God, the man should care and provide for his children, always considering their wellbeing physically, emotionally, and spiritually. He has a divine responsibility to provide security to his household financially and otherwise.

Below are eight basic needs that the man must provide for his children:

Security: Children must be given at minimum the basic survival needs, such as shelter, food, clothing, medical care, and protection from harm. Scripture regards the proper care of children as being a signage of sincere faith.

But those who won't care for their relatives, especially those in their own household, have denied the true faith. Such people are worse than unbelievers. ***(1 Timothy 5:8)***

Throughout scripture, we observe God providing the necessary sustenance for His children.

I have given them to you for food, just as I have given you grain and vegetables. ***(Genesis 9:3)***

In the same way God supplies His people's need the man must ensure his children are provided for. There is an expectation for all men who become fathers to guarantee their children a life void of unnecessary provocation. Fathers should desist from driving their children to anger provoked by wrath; instead, must provide Godly and useful instruction for them as taught in the scripture:

Fathers do not provoke your children to anger by the way you treat them. Rather, bring them up with the discipline and instruction that comes from the Lord. **(Ephesians 6:4)**

Stability: Stability comes from family and community. A child is more secure and emotionally safe when the family remains together in a permanent household. The absence of a stable home disrupts the child's life. Children in stable family structures have a sense of belonging, and cultural continuity. While the Bible does not openly condemn people who fall prey to broken relationships, the scriptures generally discourage separation. Consider the text below as Jesus explains His position on divorce.

"Haven't you read the Scriptures?" Jesus replied. "They record that from the beginning 'God made them male and female."

And he said, 'This explains why a man leaves his father and mother and is joined to his wife, and the two are united into one.' Since they are no longer two but one, let no one split apart what God has joined together." ***(Matthew 19:4-6)***

God, the designer of the nuclear family, posits that it is best to rear children in a stable household. He opines that family should be constructed on the foundation of a marriage between one faithful man and a loving woman. Unhealthy relationships entail disrespect, hurt and humiliation and often leads to divorce. Such relationship have significant impact on both parents and children. Divorce creates an unstable environment for children and could severely impact children's conduct and academic performance. Where possible parents should reconcile their differences. Every child deserves stability. It is a basic human right to live and fellowship with both parents.

Forgiveness is a necessary component in relationships; it allows for reconciliation, and complete restoration to families.

There is a direct relationship between a father's absence and children's ability to adjust and function in society. Several research suggest that the absence of fathers (regardless of the reason) is directly linked to the poor behaviour and poor performance displayed by students in school. Separation, divorce, or desertion adversely affect children's development. According to Demo and Acock (1988), parental separation, divorce, or desertion have alarming results. These include vulnerability to acute psychiatric disturbances, aversion to marriage, and proneness to divorce once they marry. The research also postulates that: Children reared in households where the two biological parents are not present will exhibit lower levels of self-esteem than their counterparts who live in nuclear families. The adverse effects on youthful well-being will be especially acute when the cause of parental absence is marital separation, divorce, or desertion.

Consistency: As the father, you should synchronise with the child's mother, ensuring important values are ingrained consistently. Grose (2018) opines that consistency means following through and doing as promised. Parents should resist giving children second and third chances when they break the rules or behave poorly around others. The same author believes a consistent approach to discipline helps to put children in control of their behaviour. He further states that a consistent approach to the implementation rules will result in them eventually doing the right thing as they know they will be held accountable.

Those who spare the rod of discipline hate their children. Those who love their children care enough to discipline them.

(Proverbs 13:24)

Emotional Support: Fathers should encourage their children to trust, respect, build self-esteem and ultimately develop independence. They should be sensitive to the feelings of their children and should endeavour to foster an environment that supports the holistic development of their children. Dads should be firm but approachable, allowing children to discuss concerns. They should celebrate them when they excel and encourage them when they do not meet expectations. Keep the bar of expectation high but scaffold them with love and support. Your words and actions matter. The Bible discourages all forms of exasperation.

Fathers do not aggravate your children, or they will become discouraged. ***(Colossians 3:21)***

Love: Our love for our children should mirror God's love for us, His people. He holds us accountable when we err, but we are confident of His unchanging and affirming love.

For the Lord disciplines those he loves, and he punishes each one he accepts as his child as you endure this divine discipline, remember that God is treating you as his own children. Who ever heard of a child who is never disciplined by its father? If

God doesn't discipline you as he does all his children, it means that you are illegitimate and are not really his children at all.

(Hebrews 12:6)

Similarly, we should correct and discipline our children in love. They should always be aware of our unalterable love. Saying and showing you love your children can help them to overcome almost any parenting 'mistakes' you might make. Even when your kids have disobeyed, angered, frustrated, and rebelled against you consistently, demonstrate your love for them. Studies show that when fathers are affectionate and supportive, it dramatically impacts the child's cognitive and social development, inspiring their self-confidence. - Pediatric Associates, 2021.

Be your Children's Model: Paediatric Associates (2021) explains that fathers influence children and how they interact with others as they grow. How fathers treat their children will influence what they look for in other people. Balcom (n.d.) concurs that many adult sons whose fathers abandoned them have difficulty developing and sustaining self-esteem, forming lasting emotional attachments, recognising their feelings, or being expressive with their adult partners and children. Fathers play a critical role in shaping the world around their children. The research shows that boys tend to model themselves after their fathers, and from a tender age, they will pursue their father's approval. Emergent literacy suggests that humans are social beings who imitate the conduct of those around them as they grow. Therefore, if a father is caring and respects people, the children, especially boys, will grow up respecting and caring for others. On the other hand, girls depend on their fathers for security and emotional support. A girl learns from her father what a good relationship with a man looks like. If a father is loving and gentle, his daughter will look for those qualities in men when she is old enough to begin dating. If a father is strong and courageous, she will relate closely to men of the same character. -*Pediatric and Associates 2018.*

Reflection:

- Think of two words to describe the relationship with your children.

Affirmations:

- I will faithfully teach and instruct my Children to walk in the ways of the Lord.

- I will lead them by both precept and example.

- I promise to make myself available to provide emotional, physical, psychological, and spiritual support to my children.

- I will endeavour to create a stable environment for my children that would facilitate proper growth and development.

- I will teach and instruct them in Biblical ways to honour God as they leave their mark in society.

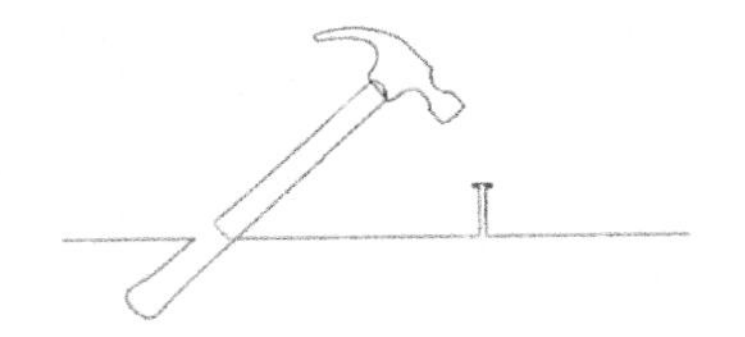

MAN, AND HIS SPOUSE

Give honour to marriage and remain faithful to one another in marriage. God will surely judge people who are immoral and those who commit adultery.

<u>***Hebrews 13:4***</u>

Under the constitution of heaven, the only legal and legitimate union is the one between one man and one woman drawn together out of love. This marriage is described as honourable, meaning God acknowledges it. Sex is only permissible within marriage, and any other form of arrangement or practice regarding sexual relations is dishonourable. The writer of Hebrew made it clear that God approves only the loving relationship between one man and one woman.

The man should also love and treat his spouse with respect, compassion, and care. To gain an insight into the validity of this text, we must examine the situational context that inspired the writing. Epistles are generally task-oriented and thus written to address a pending circumstance. At the time of the writing, there was the practice of varying sexual immoralities, including adultery. Therefore, the writer drags the believers' memory to God's expectation concerning marriage. Real mature, godly men perform actions and participate in activities informed by scripture. Any conduct outside of the parameters established by scripture is dangerous and should seize. God designed marriage; therefore, He is the authority on marriage. He has the right to pass laws and determine the policies to govern marriage. In that policy, he specified the nature of the involvement by both sexes.

This explains why a man leaves his father and mother and is joined to his wife, and the two are united into one.

(Genesis 2:24)

This text forms the basis for the new covenantal agreement, two becoming one.

For this reason, a man will leave his father and mother and be united to his wife, and the two will become one flesh.

(Matthew 19:5)

God first modelled the expectation of joining a man to a woman when he brought Eve to Adam. Having assessed the circumstances concerning Adam, He determined the best gift for Adam was a partner, woman.

Then the Lord God said, *"It is not good for the man to be alone. I will make a helper who is just right for him. So, the Lord God caused the man to fall into a deep sleep. While the man slept, the Lord God took out one of the man's ribs and closed the opening. Then the Lord God made a woman from the rib, and he brought her to the man."* ***(Genesis 2:18-22)***

We observed two foundational truths in this above text:

He brought ONE woman. God expects Adam to be faithful to one woman. With this one woman, he must enjoy sexual relations and procreate.'

He brought a WOMAN. It is crystal clear that all sexual relations should only be between a man and a woman in marriage. Whereas the scripture is vague as it relates to whether an official wedding ceremony was conducted, we are sure of one thing: God, the developer of marriage, brought the union together.

God also defined the social practices of marriage: These includes:

Be faithful to your wife. It is the responsibility of a man to be loyal to his wife, and he must view this as a high calling, especially since it is not optional.

You must not commit adultery. ***(Exodus 20:14)***

The originator of marriage brought one woman to the first man highlighting His intent for marriage and likewise defining its parameters. God's action toward the first relationship showcases His heart and desire for His people. God condemns the act of adultery (sex beyond the borders of marriage) in Exodus 20:14; thus, there is no basis or grounds on which extramarital affairs are justified. Like the times of ancient Israel, some hedonistic cultures glorify and accept extramarital affairs. God is the legislature and judiciary of His people and determines that we should not condone such immoral practices. If we engage in extramarital affairs, we violate God's laws equating to sin (transgression of God's law).

No one here has more authority than I do. He has held back nothing from me except you because you are his wife. How could I do such a wicked thing? It would be a great sin against God."

(Genesis 39:9)

As purpose-driven men, we must seek to allow scriptures to guide our actions, not culture. Any man can have multiple intimate relationships, but only an authentic, purpose-driven, and moral man can resist the easy ploys of the enemy and remain faithful to his wife.

Brothers, let us do the honourable thing: remain loyal to our marital covenants. Not only is it Godly, but it is healthy. Currie (2014), in an article entitled "Marriage: The Power of Faithfulness," shares ten compelling reasons for a man remaining faithful to his union:

- It reflects your commitment to God. Your commitment to your relationship voices your loyalty to the sovereign God.

- It is covenant to your wife. Your word is your bond. Integrity is measured and trust is awarded by your will to honour your commitment to your spouse.

- It strengthens and encourages relationships to grow. Wherever there is trust, love blossoms.

- It brings freedom and builds confidence. Jealousy erodes where loyalty emerges.

- It prevents broken hearts and frequent hurts. A healthy relational climate invites peace.

- It is a gift of strength, stability, and security to your children. Failure to make this deposit will result in costly returns.

- It will prevent or reduce your chances of swift marital decay. Medicate today to prevent future isolation.

- It furnishes your children with the right example of a healthy marriage. A culture of faithfulness creates a cycle of healthy marital seasons.

- It eliminates financial erosion. Lack of the poison that slowly kills love.

- It is the precedent for ongoing construction on your marriage. It builds and establishes stronger marriages today.

And he said, this explains why a man leaves his father and mother and is joined to his wife, and the two are united into one.' Since they are no longer two but one, let no one split apart what God has joined together. **(Matthew 19:5-6)**

Love your wife. Several pieces of research show that people in loving relationships have a lower death rate when compared to others. If a person is in a healthy, supportive relationship, they are more likely to have higher self-esteem, which lowers both men's and women's chances of becoming depressed. Therefore, a husband's action towards his wife could positively affect both persons' health and life span. It encourages harmony within the home and creates a healthy atmosphere safe and conducive to raising children. It also has the potential to reduce friction and boost the couples' financial savings, money generally spent on counselling, and other forms of damage control interventions. A person is likelier to adopt safer behaviours in an intimate, loving relationship. It also helps reduce a person's anxiety (Marion, 2014). Interestingly the word 'love' used here in the text is derived from the Greek word 'agape', which has nothing to do with erotic or emotions. The love that God expects a man to share with his wife is one in which he:

- loves without changing.
- loves in a self-giving manner.
- gives his love without demanding or expecting re-payment.
- loves so selfless that it can be given to the unlovable or unappealing.
- loves even when it is rejected.

> *For husbands, this means love your wives, just as Christ loved the church.* **(Ephesians 5:25)**

'Agape love' gives and loves because it wants to; it does not demand or expect repayment for the love given. It gives because it loves, it does not love to receive -Guzick, 2018.

- What reason do we really have to not love our spouses?

- What error is so great that makes her unworthy of your love?

Let us make a commitment to love our spouses unconditionally as we seek to fulfil our purposes as men and husbands.

Be gentle and understanding. Women need to be understood, appreciated, and loved.

Always be humble and gentle. Be patient with each other, making allowance for each other's faults because of your love. Make every effort to keep yourselves united in the Spirit, binding yourselves together with peace. **(Ephesians 4:2-3)**

Avoid treating her harshly. Women need to be cherished. The way we treat them should mirror Christ's attitude and care toward His church. As we examine Christ's nature toward His church, we notice that He is approachable and always willing to forgive, restore, and reconcile His church gently. He is merciful, compassionate, and patient. This projects the protocol for how men should treat their wives.

Husbands, love your wives and never treat them harshly.

(Colossians 3:19)

Support his wife. The husband must work closely with his wife to provide emotional and financial support for the children. Together they must provide appropriate monitoring and discipline for their children. Additionally, husbands should remain **a permanent and loving presence** in both his wife's and children's lives. Provision means much more than finances that is paying the bills. A husband must also provide his family with emotional, physical, mental, and spiritual support.

Affirm her beauty. Women want to always feel beautiful. Husbands should regularly compliment and affirms her beauty.

Husbands appreciate the physical, intellectual, emotional, and spiritual beauty of your wife. You are altogether beautiful, my darling, beautiful in every way. You are altogether beautiful, my darling, beautiful in every way. **(Songs of Solomon 4:7)**

Provide her with stability. Every woman wants to feel safe physically, emotionally, and mentally. Husbands should provide stability to his household.

Affirmations:

- I will endeavour to be faithfully committed to my spouse for life.
- I promise to treat my spouse with honour and respect.
- I will ensure the preservation of this union from all external attacks and internal decay.
- I will love my spouse unconditionally and be supportive of her.

MAN, AND HIS FELLOWSHIP WITH MAN.

But if we are living in the light, as God is in the light, then we have fellowship with each other, and the blood of Jesus, his Son, cleanses us from all sin.

1 John 1:7

At the heart of man's purpose is his relationship with his fellow man. This is so important on God's agenda that it forms the most critical prerequisite to true fellowship with God. We are relational beings, and thus a significant proportion of God's expectation for man lies in his interpersonal relationship. He is to cultivate a culture of peace and harmony, as highlighted in Jesus' Sermon on the Mount, better known as the Beatitudes.

God blesses those who work for peace, for they will be called the children of God. **(Matthew 5:29)**

Man's love for God is measured by his unconditional love for his fellow man, which is equivalent to his love for God. Therefore, he is instructed in scripture to foster a relationship with others borne out of sincere love.

And you must love the Lord your God with all your heart, all your soul, all your mind, and all your strength.' The second is equally important: 'Love your neighbour as yourself.' No other commandment is greater than these. **(Mark 12:30-31)**

This unconditional love is not limited to friends, colleagues, relatives, or family but should be disseminated to those who offend, dislike, or hate him. The love that man shares with his fellow man should transcend corridors of love and should not be given with conditionalities such as gifts, support, or mere appreciation. It must embody the selfless love of God depicted in scripture; the 'free' gift bestowed upon all men even though they are unworthy. Love is more about giving than it is about receiving. The man must purpose himself to epitomise this quality of love.

"If you love only those who love you, why should you get credit for that? Even sinners love those who love them! And if you do good only to those who do good to you, why should you get credit? Even sinners do that much! And if you lend money only to those who can repay you, why should you get credit? Even sinners will lend to other sinners for a full return. "Love your enemies! Do good to them. Lend to them without expecting to be repaid. Then your reward from heaven will be very great, and you will truly be acting as children of the Most High, for he is kind to those who are unthankful and wicked. You must be compassionate, just as your Father is compassionate.

(Luke 6:32-36)

Our contemporary world is characterised by hatred, bitterness, and wickedness, leading to the continuous destruction of lives and property, quite like Jesus' ministry on earth. Our response to the dilemma must depict Jesus' teaching. Let us be loving to all men; treat all men with the same measure of kindness that you would desire. By doing so, we can change our communities, churches, and nations one person at a time, spreading God's unconditional love.

Affirmations:

- I promise to be my brother's keeper. My life will be purpose driven.
- I will endeavour to be a support to those in need of hope and restoration.
- I commit to demonstrating compassion in my interpersonal relationships.

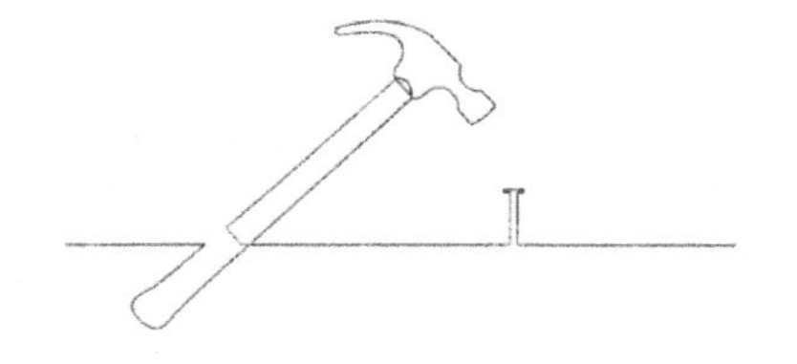

MAN, AND HIM FULFILLING GOD'S EXPECTATION

With a sacred expectation, I look for God in ALL of the circumstances of my day.

Aiden Wilson Tozer

In essence, man is created to honour God and serve Him and His mission willingly. He fulfils the key missionary expectations when he extends love to all, and positively influence his fellow men sharing the most uplifting message of hope, the gospel. Additionally, he is to take care of the earth, impacting his environment physically, morally, and positively. He should also treat his family well. The expectations and desires of people often shape our society.

Expectations are beliefs that come from people's thought process often after examining some form of evidence. Something inspires our expectation. Our expectations are not always correct because of flaws in our logic and the bias of hope and desire. Sometimes, we "get our hopes up" based on a false premise or a misreading of evidence. Often, we form expectations automatically, without conscious reasoning. When expectations are not met, pain ensues, and we often place blame on something or someone who did not live up to our expectations—even if our expectations were unreasonable. Our greatest expectation must be to fulfil God's intent. This gives rise to purpose.

'Purpose' is often defined as having many accomplishments, including varying college degrees, mansions, high-end cars, billions of dollars' worth of assets and cash, and significant scientific discoveries and inventions. While these may contribute significantly to the earth's development and preservation, 'purpose' is not limited to what we acquire; instead, it is doing what we were created for. In pursuit of greatness, we forsake some aspects of our purpose, such as family, fellowship, and our relationship with God. Our purpose cannot exclude God since we were created for His purpose. Jesus shares an account of two builders in a bid to share a valuable lesson to His audience and subsequently us:

Anyone who listens to my teaching and follows it is wise, like a person who builds a house on solid rock. Though the rain comes in torrents and the floodwaters rise and the winds beat against that house, it won't collapse because it is built on bedrock. But anyone who hears my teaching and doesn't obey it is foolish, like a person who builds a house on sand. When the rains and floods come and the winds beat against that house, it will collapse with a mighty crash. ***(Matthew 7:24-27)***

Note that both builders built a house; therefore, the issue was not what was constructed but where it was created. You can make an empire and have outstanding accomplishments worldwide but fail to fulfil your purpose. 'Purpose' is sustainable and lasting, not seasonal. If you acquire all within the world but fail to honour God, like the builder who built the house on the sand, you would have failed to build a sustainable and impactful legacy.

And what do you benefit if you gain the whole world but lose your own soul? **(Mark 8:36)**

Purpose is rooted in honouring God. The wise builder exerts his energy building a good house and on a firm rock. He didn't choose what was easy; he selected what was honourable. A wise man will seek to fulfil this high calling.

I press on to reach the end of the race and receive the heavenly prize for which God, through Christ Jesus, is calling us.

(Philippians 3: 14)

Serve purposefully and wisely. Jesus told us to expect His return—although the timing of His return is beyond our knowing. God expects us to serve excellently until He returns.

"Be ready, because the Son of Man will come at an hour when you do not expect him." **(Luke 12:40)**

God expects us to worship Him as an expression of reverence and thanksgiving to Him. He also expects us to be obedient. He wants us to not only love Him but to act justly toward each other and to show love and compassion to others.

Affirmations:

- I will honour God by ably representing him before others.

- I will be known for my track record of good deeds and an exemplary lifestyle. I will live a life that is worthy of emulating.

- I will teach by both precept and example the behavioural values that I want to be instilled within my child.

- I will be the type of man that I want my sons to emulate and pattern and the example of the type of man that my daughters should marry.

- I promise to leave my parents (physically, financially, and emotionally) and cleave to my wife.

- I promise to exercise the biblical model of submission (mutual).

- I will ensure that this relationship is the most significant of all human relationships.

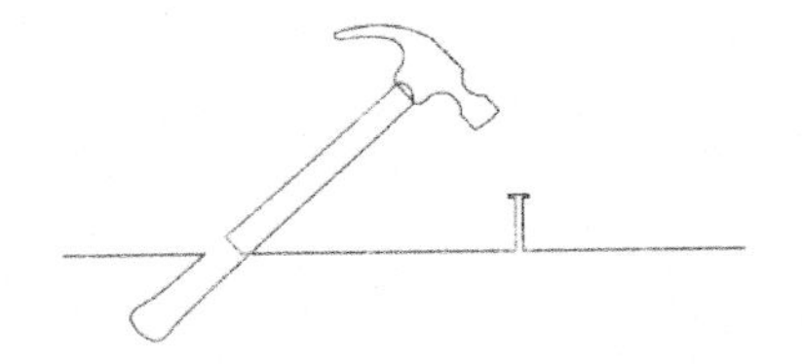

MAN, AND HIS FAITH

Let us hold tightly without wavering to the hope we affirm, for God can be trusted to keep his promise.

<u>Hebrew 10:23</u>

The Biblical records shows that the first thing God did after creating man was to "give him dominion and care for His marvellous creation".

The Lord God placed the man in the Garden of Eden to tend and watch over it. ***(Genesis 2:15)***

There is no Biblical account of Adam asking God: how will I do this? I have never undergone tertiary training, nor do I have any experience in leadership and administration. He accepted God's word and began to function in his leadership capacity. Faith is doing what God says simply because He says it. Adam was aware that God built the garden he lived in, planted the trees, provided the water, positioned the animals in the garden, and gave flight routes to the birds. ***See Genesis 2:8-15.***

Then the Lord God planted a garden in Eden in the east, and there he placed the man he had made. The Lord God made all sorts of trees grow up from the ground—trees that were beautiful and that produced delicious fruit. In the middle of the garden, he placed the tree of life and the tree of the knowledge of good and evil. A river flowed from the land of Eden, watering the garden, and then dividing into four branches. The first branch, called the Pishon, flowed around the entire land of Havilah, where gold is found. The gold of that land is exceptionally pure; aromatic resin and onyx stone are also found there. The second branch, called the Gihon, flowed around the entire land of Cush. The third branch, called the Tigris, flowed east of the land of Asshur. The fourth branch is called the Euphrates.

Such an unquestionable and undisputable reputation, coupled with the simple fact that He is God and whatever He spoke was manifested, became the launching pad for Adam to believe God. Faith is the firm persuasion and relentless confidence in God and what God says. The evidence of what is not seen and the mere fact that we cannot exist without God is enough to spur man to believe God for the unseen, unknown, and unheard. Faith is an expression of complete trust in someone or something. It is founded on the premise of who spoke and the details that are available concerning the one who spoke.

The man was created to believe God and His promises. As we examine the text concerning the first man and his interaction with God, we note that faith is the product of relationship. It is impossible to believe God and His promises when we do not share a relationship with Him. This relationship allowed for frequent dialogues and communion. A relationship with God allows you to learn about God and His expectation and inspires to believe Him.

But the Lord God warned him, "You may freely eat the fruit of every tree in the garden— except the tree of the knowledge of good and evil. If you eat its fruit, you are sure to die."

(Genesis 2:16-17)

Relationships provide the platform to come to grips with His expectations. Therefore, fellowship is the fundamental basis for faith in God. Adam learned what God expected and was able to act because of His relationship with God. Faith is the outcome of a process of frequent consultation, discovering, and performing that which He expects.

Like Adam, in our quest to trust God, we must build concrete and sustainable relationship through constant study of His word and consistent dialogue (prayer). When we study His word, we know what He expects and can better trust Him in fulfilling His expectations.

I have hidden your word in my heart, that I might not sin against you. **(Psalms 119:11)**

Faith maximises within a covenantal relationship with God, knowing that our welfare and well-being are His immediate responsibilities. The Word of God helps to renew the covenant and reminds us of its never-ending benefits. Guzick (2018) posits that a renewed confidence in the greatness of God and his Covenant will make us stand strong in the faith. Faith in God should be one without wavering. The word wavering is coined from the Greek word 'aklines', meaning not leaning or inclining, firm and unmovable. Man must therefore seek to cultivate complete faith in God and what He says. There is no room for faith to bend or move. It should be firm and sustained. We see the severe consequence of the first man Adam who was inconsistent in His faithfulness to God and His commands. It is untrue to think that Adam did not believe God, but it is evident that this faith moved to the point of persuasion.

The woman was convinced. She saw that the tree was beautiful, and its fruit looked delicious, and she wanted the wisdom it would give her. So, she took some of the fruit and ate it. Then she gave some to her husband, who was with her, and he ate it, too. At that moment their eyes were opened, and they suddenly felt shame at their nakedness. ***(Genesis 3:6-7)***

For faith to remain intact, it must be serviced through prayer and the constant reminder of God's promise (The Word). Let us hasten to correct some misconceptions about faith and what it entails:

- Faith is not limited to, though it expresses positive thinking.

- Faith is about doing what God says because you believe God.

- Faith does not foster thoughts of excuses neither does it seek out opportunities to avoid honouring God's expectations.

- Faith is a true representation of the heart and its desire therefore it does not mean that the man should pretend to be unchallenged. Instead, it should prompt him to express his weakness to God and trust Him for a resolution.

- Faith is the unquestionable confidence in God and that which we hope for and the assurance that the Lord is working, even though we cannot see it.

- Faith knows that no matter what the situation is, in our lives or someone else's, the lord is working on it.

It is the act whereby the man lays hold of God's resources, becomes obedient to what He has prescribed and putting aside all self-interest and self-reliance, trusts Him completely. (Advancing God's Kingdom: Living by Faith, n.d.)

There are five fundamental intents of unwavering faith:

Faith is necessary for God: *Faith shows the reality of what we hope for; it is the evidence of things we cannot see.*

(Hebrews 11:1)

Faith moves God to act: *If you need wisdom, ask our generous God, and he will give it to you. He will not rebuke you for asking. But when you ask him, be sure that your faith is in God alone. Do not waver, for a person with divided loyalty is as unsettled as a wave of the sea that is blown and tossed by the wind. Such people should not expect to receive anything from the Lord.* ***(James 1:5-7)***

Faith gives us strength when we faced with trials and tests: *For you know that when your faith is tested, your endurance has a chance to grow.* ***(James 1:3)***

Faith motivates what we do: *Just as the body is dead without breath, so also faith is dead without good works.* ***(James 2:26)***

Faith encourages others: *We always pray for you, and we give thanks to God, the Father of our Lord Jesus Christ. For we have heard of your faith in Christ Jesus and your love for all of God's people.* ***(Colossians 1:3-4)***

Faith is the foundational ingredient necessary for

establishing a relationship with God. It is the assurance that the promise revealed through the Word of God is genuine despite it being unseen or unheard. Therefore, faith is not correlated to what is seen through our physical eyes or heard through our feeble ears but rather what we believe.

Our inability or reluctance to believe God will automatically subscribe to believing in ourselves or the promises of others. Unfortunately, Adam trusted in the persuasion of his wife, birthed from the lies of the enemy instead of God's word.

The serpent was the shrewdest of all the wild animals the Lord God had made. One day he asked the woman, "Did God really say you must not eat the fruit from any of the trees in the garden? Of course, we may eat fruit from the trees in the garden," the woman replied. "It's only the fruit from the tree in the middle of the garden that we are not allowed to eat. God said, 'You must not eat it or even touch it; if you do, you will die.'" "You won't die!" the serpent replied to the woman. "God knows that your eyes will be opened as soon as you eat it, and you will be like God, knowing both good and evil. "The woman was convinced. She saw that the tree was beautiful, and its fruit looked delicious, and she wanted the wisdom it would give her. So, she took some of the fruit and ate it. Then she gave some to her husband, who was with her, and he ate it, too.

(Genesis 3:1-7)

Within contemporary society, one of the criteria for proving something credible is the ability to present tangible and verifiable evidence. The evidence is then ratified to determine its authenticity. Once verified, it is classified as being truthful. Not so with God. He does not need to provide any supporting details to determine the validity of His promises made in scripture. His character is all the evidence required. Once the man hears the instruction, he is to act. The word 'hears' which is derived from 'shema' in Hebrew is an action word which means to hear and to move to action, forsaking any need to evaluate the truthfulness of the command. Just as Adam heard God's word giving him dominion to rule over and name all the creatures in the garden, he was expected to resist the temptation of partaking in the forbidden fruit, having heard God's initial instruction. Adam's faith was inconsistent and thus resulted in the ultimate fall of humanity. A man's faith in God must always be firm and consistent. Your purpose, integrity, family, and those you serve, depend on your unwavering faith in God and His Word. Interestingly, Eve ate the fruit, and there were no noticeable changes, but the moment Man partook, they realised they were naked. The man is the head; thus, when all others waver in faith, he must cultivate faith in God and His word. There is no excuse for living outside of God's covenantal order.

So, my dear brothers and sisters, be strong and immovable. Always work enthusiastically for the Lord, for you know that nothing you do for the Lord is ever useless.

(1 Corinthians 15:58)

Lack of faith does not always mean that we are responding to something negative but instead that we are reacting negatively toward God and His word. Noticed that the serpent told Eve that "God knows that your eyes will be opened as soon as you eat it, and you will be like God, knowing both good and evil." (Genesis 3:5). This is the charge God laid against the man in the text below.

Then the Lord God said, "Look, the human beings have become like us, knowing both good and evil. ***(Genesis 3:22)***

Trusting is about loving Him so much that you do as He expects always. Whether we actively or passively refute God's promise, we violate His expectation.

Therefore, faith is the tangible evidence that God's Word is accurate, and our will to believe it will yield the promise attached to it. We possess palpable proof of things that are not yet visible.

Reflection:

- To what extent do you TRUST God?

Affirmations:

- I promise to be faithful to the God that has called me.

- I will trust his words to provide the basic direction for my life.

- I affirm my confidence in God's ability to be faithful even when I am faithless.

- I promise to balance the concepts of investment, consumption, and storage to optimise wealth creation.

- I will believe God that even when negative things present, that in all things God is working for my Good.

- I promise never to betray the trust that has been reposed in me.

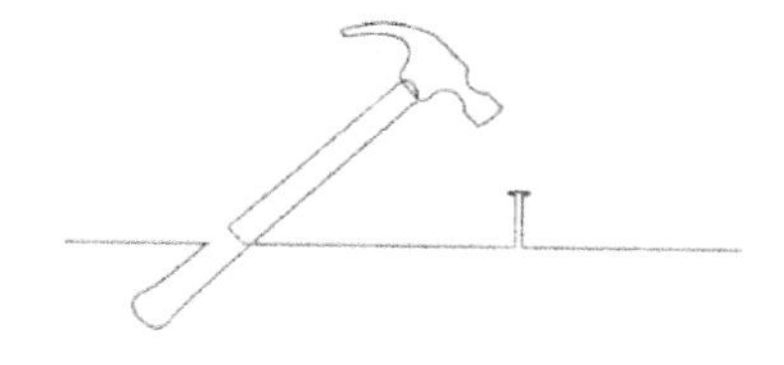

MAN, AND HIS LEADERSHIP

The head of every man is Christ, the head of woman is man, and the head of Christ is God.

1 Corinthians 11:3b

God designed the framework of order, authority, and accountability, not culture. Therefore, the principles of order, authority, and accountability precede the idea of a patriarchal society dating back to the Garden of Eden when God made the first man and woman. 'Head,' when translated from the word 'kephale', generally means master, source, or lord of. Paul, in the text, seeks to highlight God's hierarchical order:

- ✓ God
- ✓ Jesus
- ✓ Man
- ✓ Wife

Let us examine the statement as it is used in this context. 'Head' implies 'source,' meaning a place or person from which a thing or person originates. Therefore, contextually the first woman came from man, the man from Jesus, and Jesus from God. If a person comes from another, the original person has authority over the derivative, and the derivative is accountable to that person as its source. In essence, the word 'head' used in the text sought to outline the order set up by God based on the idea that the woman came from man, similarly to the man serving Jesus since he came from Jesus. Jesus also served His Father with dignity because He came from His Father, God. On this basis, the woman is accountable to the man, the man is responsible to Christ, and Christ is accountable to God. Whomever you are indebted to has authority over you.

For the first man didn't come from woman, but the first woman came from man. And man was not made for woman, but woman was made for man. **(1 Corinthians 11:8-9)**

This pattern lays out the order that God intended from the beginning. Note that the woman was made to support the man and not the man for the woman. Therefore, headship speaks to authority, meaning that the man has the appropriate responsibility to lead and the authority to hold those he led accountable. Guzick (2018) contends that it is suitable for the woman to submit to the man who is her head, as man is expected to submit to Christ in the same manner that Christ submits to His father. As the woman submits to her husband, he must lead in a godly, discipline, and respectable manner worthy of her submission. Leadership begins with a vision, the ability to think about or plan the future with imagination or wisdom." Robertson and Rodney (2021) further posit that vision is a mental portrait of a preferable future, the perception of the future in reverse, requiring pragmatic steps to be realised. Vision creates a path for others to follow and serves as a critical light offering hope in the darkest moments. Therefore, one must carefully craft a mental idea of where he sees his family in the future. This vision must be formulated through prayer and encapsulate God's vision for our lives. As the man, we must lead our families as God leads His church. A wife will find it easier to submit to leadership guided by a vision defined in God's will. God's vision for His church transcends beyond spirituality to areas such as finance, welfare, well-being, health, fellowship, fun, and family. Like God, we must prayerfully develop a holistic vision that reflects God's nature. Engraved in that vision is the team, the man, and the family, all working for a shared and meaningful outcome. The idea of a team eliminates any thought of a person being subservient or bossy. The concept of a team concretises that all team members are essential and play a vital yet distinct role in pursuing a thriving marriage.

The roles of the man and woman are unique and are not meant to be imitated by the other. Some hold the view that all members of the team are equal and function in the same capacity. Any institution that operates without order, including marriage, is prone to chaos. Chaos and confusion are eliminated when a structure is applied to the context. Whereas all roles are significant, and none is to be viewed as superior to others, it is insane to have the members performing the same tasks and serving in the same capacity. The writers of this book are avid supporters of football, a team sport. During each game, eleven players are appointed to play with the sole goal of winning, each fulfilling critical roles necessary for the team's success. While they fulfil their unique assignment, the 'forward' may need to run back to the point of defence to support the defender, but this does not make him the defender.

Similarly, the wife is not competing against her husband (for the "most important" role); instead, she is working assiduously to support him. By doing so, the family fulfils its mission. Goals are realised when all parties are cognisant of the aim and are aware of their role in fulfilling the mission and where they are enthusiastically passionate about the task to be completed. One of the central tenets of successful and effective leadership is providing a clear focus for the team members, and the family. The leader must develop the art and science of effective communication and use every opportunity to keep the family abreast of the unit's goals. Since communication is only complete with feedback, he must carefully listen to the other team members and acknowledge the value of their input.

If you make listening and observation your occupation, you will gain much more than you can by talking. - *Robert Baden-Powell*

The leader must foster a culture of consulting God before proceeding with any task. Always invite the family to pray before undertaking decisions. Remember, we are tasked to be head as Christ is head of the church. One noticeable observation with the model of Christ's leadership is that He always took time to pray. Prayer is a response to an invitation to discuss important matters with the sovereign God. Thus, we are shareholders within the Kingdom of God. We are on His Team; therefore, regular consultation with Him is imperative.

Trust in the Lord with all your heart; do not depend on your own understanding. Seek his will in all you do, and he will show you which path to take. **(Proverbs 5:6)**

Communication is an effective tool for inclusion, and support is best garnered when one incorporates all the team members. It is a powerful way to show how much you value the members of your family and what they have to say.

It is easier to reach our potential when we learn the value of including others in our quest. - John Wooden

Including your family is the secret to stimulating their interest and prompting them to support the vision; that is the one they helped to construct instead of the one they were handed. Also, this involvement reinforces the idea that all team members are valuable to the process. Your wife offers more than just taking instruction; she contributes to the discourse by collectively assessing and helping to fix discrepancies. Your job is not to boss your wife around and get her to conform to your instructions. Instead, it is to rediscover the purpose of the dining table as the place where you interact and clarify critical concerns, resolve conflicts, and make crucial decisions. One of the most incredible sights in this world is a man in fellowship with his family.

"The dinner table is the centre for the teaching and practicing not just of table manners but of conversation, consideration, tolerance, family feeling, and just about all the other accomplishments of polite society except the minute."

- *Judith Martin*

Through discussion, your wife will discover new ways to support you better and boost the synergy within the union. In this sense, the wife (Eve) is described in scripture as a help meet.

The term help meet is translated from the Hebrew phrase 'ezer kenegdo', meaning perfect and suitable for Adam. Eve had the right qualities and skills to work alongside Adam to fulfil God's mission, and she was created to help him. Wrapped up in her purpose was the ability to deliver quality support. However, for Eve to provide the best support for Adam, she must possess qualities such as vision (a clear focus) and effective communication. She also needed to frequently monitor, engage in regular discussions, and provide a meaningful evaluation.

If the man is going to lead his family effectively, he must be reliant on God and apt to learn. Guiding one's family is best achieved when one enacts and initiates a plan in conjunction with God's plan.

"A man who does not plan long ahead will find trouble at his door." – Confucius

At the heart of his plan must be the will of God. An effective leader is accountable to God and thus is expected to serve in a manner that is in keeping with the nature of God as laid out in scripture.

We can make our plans, but the Lord determines our steps.

(Proverbs 16:9)

The best way to correct malpractice and offer guidance is to exemplify the desired behaviour. It is a common belief among traditional Westerners, especially men, that children should merely follow instructions and advice, thinking these shapes their character. However, it is the modelling of the expected behaviour that serves as a more effective teacher. The more desirable the model is to the observer, the more likely that model will be imitated. Conforming does not equate to submission; any attempt at coercing compliance will be short-lived. Children live what they learn.

Men occupy the prestigious place of influence and are best placed to inspire their children and empower their wives, starting with becoming the icon of purpose, productivity, and performance. These three criteria are the rubric for assessing our responsibility, i.e., priest, protector, and provider. They are critical components of our purpose as leaders, and they are Godly in principle and are useable as we try to influence them as role models. Becoming a priest, protector, and provider creates a meaningful framework to inspire other men within the marketplace to imitate.

...let your good deeds shine out for all to see, so that everyone will praise your heavenly Father. **(*Matthew 5:13*)**

Men should aspire to be Godly examples possessing good qualities and socialise children and others to cultivate like characteristics thus creating a healthy culture.

And you should imitate me, just as I imitate Christ.

(*1 Corinthians 11:1*)

Performance is how well we harvest moral qualities and the degree to which we exhibit those behaviours. By doing so we become a society of leaders that makes it difficult for immorality to survive.

Affirmations:

- I will trust the God that superintends the process. I will demonstrate unwavering commitment to God and by extension His words.

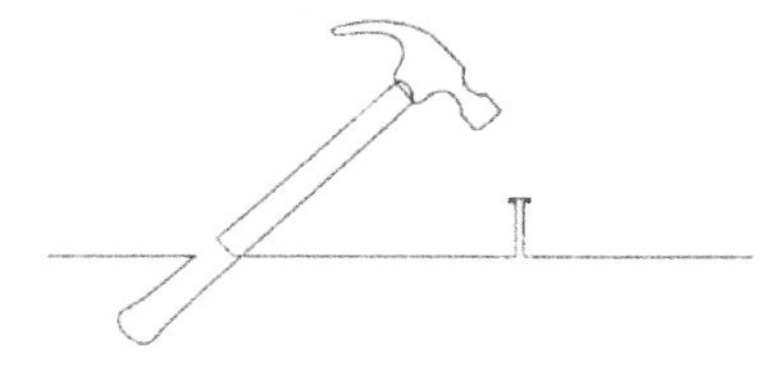

MAN, AND HIS ROLE AS PARTNER

When we see persons of worth, we should think of equalling them; when we see persons of a contrary character, we should turn inwards and examine ourselves.

Confucius

The man as head does not mean his wife is weak or incapable of God. Although God assigns man as the head, marriage is about a partnership, i.e., two people working assiduously to honour God. Like any successful corporation, marriage needs order and structure. God creates the organisational chart for the family hierarchy with Himself as the executive leader. He assigns the man the middle management role in guiding the daily operations, supporting his wife, displaying Godly qualities, and providing well-needed aid to his family. As the leader, the man should oversee his family's well-being, engage them in frequent dialogue, book regular appointments with God through prayer, and consult God on and about everything.

Trust in the Lord with all your heart; do not depend on your own understanding. Seek his will in all you do, and he will show you which path to take. ***(Proverbs 3:5-6)***

The man is the leader appointed by God appoints; however, productive leadership is the outcome of him recognising the value of his wife and working collaboratively to maximise productivity, thus creating a thriving union. A partnership is pertinent in the relationship. Hence, Peter encourages mutual submission because resistance of any size or kind and by any gender is unfruitful.

And further, submit to one another out of reverence for Christ.

(Ephesians 5:21)

Defend your family and its values always. The culture around us is always evolving. It often invites us to embrace new philosophies, practices, and norms that contradict our faith and Christly expectations. Do not allow emerging cultures to destroy your union or distort your children. Stand up and lead your family as God intends. Schools can change curricula, governments may alter laws, and society might develop new practices. Still, man must never accept immorality within the home—partner with your wife to eradicate misplaced conduct and beliefs that erode family values. Your children must know you are ready to fight for them, their well-being, and their faith, irrespective of the cost. You must never retreat; employ faith and always submit to God your King regardless of the consequence.

But if you refuse to serve the Lord, then choose today whom you will serve. Would you prefer the gods your ancestors served beyond the Euphrates? Or will it be the gods of the Amorites in whose land you now live? But as for me and my family, we will serve the Lord. The people replied, "We would never abandon the Lord and serve other gods. ***(Joshua 24:15)***

We lead best when we love most. Jesus Christ is our supreme example of leadership through love. God's word teaches that men should love their wives as Christ loved His church. Our leadership should be founded and built on love.

For husbands, this means love your wives, just as Christ loved the church. ***(Ephesians 5:25)***

Let us boldly love our wives without reservation; treat them with respect and honour. Never permit your environment to influence you to mistreat your partner. Men loving and respecting their wives is still acceptable.

Our lives should be a mission of hope to others. Waresak (2016) states, "Every great leader pursues a higher calling and purpose that transcends his own life." The writer also posits that we are positioned in this time and space to serve God for a purpose far beyond our lives. Jesus Christ, during His tenure on earth, demonstrated living beyond Himself. He cared for the poor, loved unconditionally, provided for the less fortunate, and extended compassion to the undeserving. He sought suitable moments to teach others fundamental principles about His kingdom and ways. We must use every opportunity to establish the truth through thorough teaching and the purposeful application of God's word. We must demonstrate empathy for others and actively support others. Modelling this in our household will create a culture of compassion for others.

He said to them, "Go into all the world and preach the gospel to all creation. ***(Mark 16:15)***

Manhood is engraved into our character and our actions. The 'person' cannot be separated from his traits or purpose. A man cannot comprehend his worth unless he understands his purpose. Our actions and the personality we possess defines us. Those closest to us often assign us nicknames based on our dispositions and actions, not our qualifications or vast experiences. Actions speak volumes. Therefore, we must become lifelong learners, continually seeking ways (those in keeping with scripture) to improve ourselves. We must strive to live based on the message we preach. If we are poor at managing time, resources, and money, suggesting we are good stewards is improper; similarly, if we engage in illicit sexual activities or pornography, we cannot claim to be transformed. Abusing our wives physically, emotionally, and mentally and treating them harshly are not the desired traits of a loving husband. It is hard to correct our children when we have not updated our own character flaws.

Do not judge others, and you will not be judged. For you will be treated as you treat others. The standard you use in judging is the standard by which you will be judged. "And why worry about a speck in your friend's eye when you have a log in your own? How can you think of saying to your friend, 'Let me help you get rid of that speck in your eye,' when you can't see past the log in your own eye? Hypocrite! First get rid of the log in your own eye; then you will see well enough to deal with the speck in your friend's eye. **(Matthew 7:1-5)**

Leading our families requires us to embody the Godly qualities. As Christ, we must be loving, compassionate, kind, patient, supportive, approachable, sensitive to the needs of others, protective, charitable, provide for our households and set good examples for our family.

Pursue righteousness and a godly life, along with faith, love, perseverance, and gentleness. **(1 Timothy 6:11)**

Reflection:

- What is your vision for your family?
- To what extent is that vision inspired by God?
- How do you intend to garner support for your vision?
- What type of leader are you? *Example: Transformational, authoritarian, democratic, laisser-faire.*
- How important is submission in a relationship?

Let Us Start the Process Today.

Lord, I confess I have not always led as you expected. I have erred in my role as a steward of my family, but today I crave your help. Lord, below are my struggles:

Please help me to overcome them. Lead me to the right aids that can assist. I will continue to trust you through the process to become the man I was created to be.

Amen.

Affirmations:

- I believe that in the original construction of man that God ordained him to lead.

- I recognise my God ordained role in the earth and will submit to being trained and developed to respond appropriately.

- I believe that I was endowed with the ability to make choices and will use this ability to glorify God.

- I affirm that my example of true leadership is based on the testimony of scriptures.

- I will teach my children financial management skills and ensure the development and perpetuation of generational wealth.

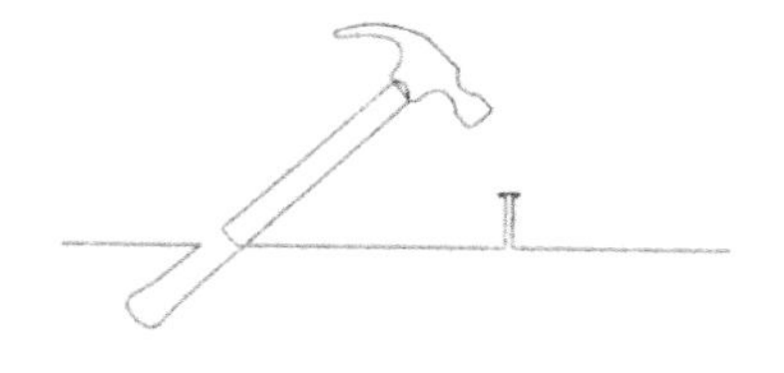

MAN, AND HIS PRAYER LIFE

One day Jesus told his disciples a story to show that they should always pray and never give up.

Luke 18:1

The original man was wired with the ability to communicate with his sovereign creator. In the original construct of man's creation, he was made in the image of God so he could relate to God, unlike any other thing created by God. The uniqueness of man was seen in how God made and brought him to life. We see his 'personal touch and involvement' explicitly stating the relationship he expected to share with the man. Man's life is intertwined with his God. Consequently, he should regularly interact with His God. A lack of prayer demonstrates a lack of faith and a lack of trust in God's Word. Man was fashioned to interact with God.

"Then the Lord God formed the man from the dust of the ground. He breathed the breath of life into the man's nostrils, and the man became a living person". ***(Genesis 2:7)***

Man is endowed explicitly with two indispensable tools: the power of **speech** and **thought,** which are necessary for active communication. Prayer must be deemed an interactive process where both parties (man and God) reserve the right to speak and be heard and then listen to and respond. The manufacturer (God) developed the product (man) with unique capabilities allowing lifetime relationships driven by his (man) capacity to choose and not coercion. Prayer is one of the most potent and intimate relational tools, and man can engage with God in the most private matters. At the beginning of Eden, prayer was a medium intended for communication and fellowship. The man was never sick, therefore, didn't require healing. He had everything he needed;

consequently, didn't need to ask for provisions. However, with the consequent fall of man, other needs began to surface and, over time, began to dominate the relational intent of prayer. Christ's intervention repaired the distortion in our relationship; we can pray like pre-fall citizens. There can be no return to God without a return to prayer. No man is more significant than his prayer life. Man must therefore recognise his responsibility to maintain active communication with God. God is always ready to communicate (talk and listen). Do you have the time to engage with him in quality conversations? Since man is an intentional product of God's creation, he will find his most incredible meaning (a sense of purpose) in communicating with God. Prayer is both affirming and empowering; it provides a supernatural lift for the soul as we become unburdened by our transparency and willingness to receive help.

A man's prayer life gives him a tremendous sense of identity as he forges a relationship with the God in whose image and likeness he was made. There can be no godliness without maintaining consistent communication with God. Prayer is one of the factors that uniquely sets man apart from all His other creations. Only man, who was formed from God's very breath, can communicate with his creator from the depth of his soul. Through prayer, he develops a strong interpersonal relationship with God. Now let's examine the qualities of effective praying.

Prayer Must Become Our Priority.

Christ prayed publicly and privately. He saw it as an opportunity to commune with His father. Praying is always appropriate.

You can ask for anything in my name, and I will do it, so that the Son can bring glory to the Father. **(John 14:13)**

Jesus, by His multiple and frequent engagements with God, modelled the importance of prioritising prayer. Interaction with God was a regular feature of His life, and communication with God was paramount for Jesus. Every time Jesus prayed, His disciples witnessed Him receiving an answer from God. It was clear that He did nothing without the Father's authorisation. Seeking God first is always in your best interest. If we prioritise prayer, God will prioritise our needs. prioritising prayer shows the extent to which we trust God. You cannot love and serve God unconditionally and not pray regularly and purposefully.

Prayer must be deemed the prime concern for man, and man must consciously realise his need for God. Since prayer connects man to God, no other relationship can supersede the bond between God and man. Man must therefore focus on building and enhancing this most intimate association. Choose to pray today and tomorrow forever.

Prayer Must Be Offered Consistently.

Man must recognise that prayer is not an event but a process to maintain a solid relationship with God. The example Christ sets out in His approach to prayer must become our practice model. So consistent was His approach to prayer that it inspired the disciple to ask Him to teach them to pray.

And it came to pass, that, as he was praying in a certain place, when he ceased, one of his disciples said unto him, Lord, teach us to pray, as John also taught his disciples. **(Luke 11:1)**

Consistency in prayer is in no way suggesting that God is reluctant and needs frequent reminders but rather the persistent nature of the faith of the man seeking God. It indicates the strength of the relationship; he enjoys and desires to see God's will done. To be 'consistent' is to be steady in doing the same thing over and over, the same way repeatedly. Consistent praying is borne out of confidence in the Entity (God) being prayed to. Constant trust leads to habitual praying. Consistent praying is done not merely out of a sense of duty but of reverence for God and the relationship one share with Him. It is giving attention to prayer with every opportunity presented. Consistent praying is praying at regular intervals, not praying non-stop, thus maintaining an attitude of praying. Prayer becomes your first and last resort.

Pray without ceasing. ***(1 Thessalonians 5:17)***

This ongoing dialogue with God requires a high level of discipline, precisely what the creator desires and honours. Consistency must become the hallmark of man's personal engagement and involvement with God. Rest assured that God is not bothered by our frequent treks to Him but instead welcomes it. Consistency indicates the depth of the relationship and the value attached to these most intimate moments with God.

Prayer Must Be Offered Persistently.

The idea of persistent prayer is borne out of being unrelenting, determined, and resolute. It means to continue praying despite the challenges, oppositions, and difficulties. The man of prayer must advocate with a level of audacity, not giving in to discouragement. This is not the kind of prayer that bends to pressure but thrives amid adversity. Jesus encourages this attitude towards praying in the Parable of the:

- Persistent Widow and the Unjust Judge Luke 18:1-8.
- Friend at Midnight Luke 11:5-13.

In the case of the persistent widow, hers was a cry for justice borne out of a sense of entitlement and a need to resolve an impending matter. She was adamant that giving up was not an option she would entertain. When no one would be her advocate, she dared to self-represent. You must never be too embarrassed to ask. Bear in mind that the greatest deterrent to prayer is unoffered prayer.

It is also essential that we demonstrate persistence when seeking redress on behalf of another. In the parable concerning the friend at midnight, he was willing to go to whatever lengths necessary to obtain his desire.

In both cases, the lesson taught is that prayer is never complete until God answers. As men, your advocacy in prayer should always be borne out of a need for justice where truth triumphs over error, right over wrong, and good over evil. Being God's legal representatives on the earth, you cannot be silent or indifferent to the injustices meted out by some people in our society. You must pray without losing hope or becoming discouraged; sometimes, it may require putting your own situations aside to solicit divine intervention for another.

Prayer Must Be Offered Passionately.

Passion should inspire praying. Man cannot have meaningful engagement with what he is not passionate about. Passion is intertwined with man's relationship with God and is not merely a request for more zeal but the outcome of his close relationship with his maker. Praying passionately entails man becoming inspired to pray because of his strong desire to see God's will done.

Our Father in heaven, may your name be kept holy. May your Kingdom come soon. May your will be done on earth as it is in heaven. ***(Matthew 6:9-10)***

This prayer is deeply rooted in man's love for God and motivates him to lay all his concerns before God while anticipating his involvement.

Elijah's prayer was effective because of his passion. He had a heart devoted to the things of God, and he was unswerving in his desire to communicate with God. He demonstrated the utmost devotion and sincerity.

Confess your sins to each other and pray for each other so that you may be healed. The earnest prayer of a righteous person has great power and produces wonderful results. Elijah was as human as we are, and yet when he prayed earnestly that no rain would fall, none fell for three and a half years!

(James 5:16-17)

Passionate praying means taking the initiative and responsibility to feel the burden of the situation and praying fervently with a firm conviction concerning the intended outcome. That unquenchable desire finds its expression in praying with urgency and resolve.

Prayer Becomes Our Shield to Adversity.

A prayer shield is effectively praying for the safety and security of others. It entails coming to God in an intercessory mode, driven by the needs of others and the great dimension to which his heart is moved to represent them in prayer. It is consciously acknowledging that others need to have the same connection, representation, and opportunity that you share with God. Representing others in prayer is not a one-event but frequently presenting individuals and their needs before a sovereign God for His intervention, provision, preservation, and protection. In the Book of Job, we see a vivid example where Job consistently interceded on behalf of his family. He was conscious of the enemy's plans to influence the behaviour of his household. He understood the sovereignty of God and His graciousness and was willing to mediate for their forgiveness in case they had violated any of God's principles. Intercession involves praying for the underserved, and prayer shield means serving God by praying for people's safety and well-being rather than their destruction. The man must never shirk his responsibility to pray.

When these celebrations ended—sometimes after several days—Job would purify his children. He would get up early in the morning and offer a burnt offering for each of them. For Job said to himself, "Perhaps my children have sinned and have cursed God in their hearts." This was Job's regular practice.

(Job 1:5)

Despite Saul's many wayward decisions, Samuel was concerned about Him and consistently offered prayers on his behalf. The prophet recognised the need for continuous prayer and advocacy for the king. Even when those in leadership fail to submit to God's leadership, man must still offer prayerful support.

As for me, I will certainly not sin against the LORD by ending my prayers for you. And I will continue to teach you what is good and right. **(1 Samuel 12:23)**

Paul encouraged his readers to pray for those that are in authority continuously. He encouraged them to pray for their well-being and prosperity to live a quiet, successful, and peaceable life in all godliness and honesty. When leaders make meaningful decisions, we subsequently benefit. Therefore, we should partner with God for their deliverance from the oppressive regime of sin. All men everywhere are obligated to engage in prayer.

I exhort therefore, that, first, supplications, prayers, intercessions, and giving of thanks, be made for all men; For kings, and for all that are in authority; that we may lead a quiet and peaceable life in all godliness and honesty.

(1 Timothy 2:1-2)

The prayer shield is the support we offer others as we unceasingly pray on their behalf.

Personal Prayer Is Expected.

Man must find a regular time for communing with God. No man is exempt from this unique experience. Jesus says when you pray rather than if you pray, implying that you must do (Matthew 6:5). The creator God craves continuous and positive interactions with his creation where you find Him whether you seek to engage in a physical location or simply the privacy of your hearts. God will compensate the time you dedicate fervent prayer with strength, provision, and protection.

Personal time for prayer facilitates man's personal enlightenment and spiritual growth, allowing him to be one with the creator and be truly transparent. No concern is unworthy of discussion, nor should it be withheld; nothing is too demeaning or inappropriate to share with God. He desires for you to be sincere and open.

Personal prayer time allows the man to share his most unique and intimate human issues without being constrained by the presence of others. Through this special allowance, he progressively gets to know God and becomes confident that God is familiar with him and his needs. Like Jacob, these interactions bring man face to face with his God as he solicits transformation. God will never turn His back on a sincere and honest seeker.

Being prayed for is critically important, but nothing replaces the need for man's private interactions with God. Man must have an intimate moment with a personable God; his spiritual and physical advancement is linked to his one-on-one moments with God.

But when you pray, go away by yourself, shut the door behind you, and pray to your Father in private. Then your Father, who sees everything, will reward you. ***(Matthew 6:6)***

For a more in debt understanding of prayer, consider registering for our six-week course on **"Critical Keys for Effective Praying"** and purchasing our detailed book entitled: **Critical Keys for Effective Praying**. This book parallels our journal: Conversation with God: A Journey to Effective Praying. Details regarding signing up for our six-weeks programs can be obtained at the rear of this book.

Affirmations:

- I believe that prayer is the number one means of establishing and maintaining a relationship with God.
- I will always ensure that my prayer time is always a priority.
- I will pray persistently and passionately. I will ensure that in prayer I not only speak but learn to listen.
- I will follow the instructions I receive from God during my moments of prayer or because of the outcome of prayer.
- I realise that Godliness is synonymous with prayerfulness.

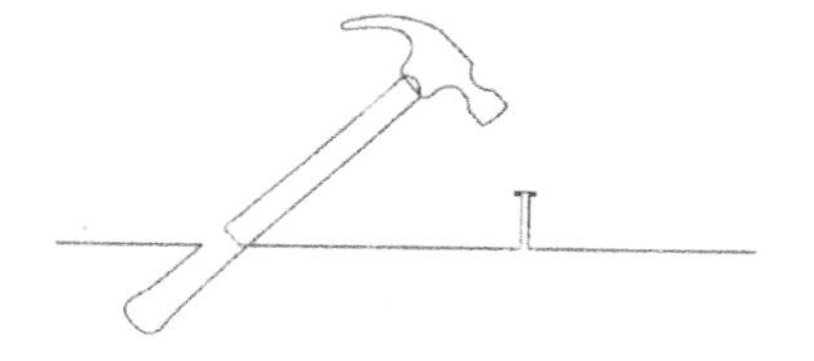

MAN, AND HIS MONEY

It is not the man who has too little, but the man who craves more, that is poor.

<u>*Seneca*</u>

A man's wealth is determined by the number of assets he possesses. Assets, therefore, determine the man's value, the greater the asset, the more valuable the man. Influence is a by-product of value. The man who possesses great value earns the right to rule and to influence decision-making. Power is a gift in the hands of a man who owns value. The higher your value, the greater the power you have. The text teaches that God made the earth with trees, animals, fishes, and birds, not cash. Assets are worth more than physical or electronic currency.

Then the Lord God planted a garden in Eden in the east, and there he placed the man he had made. The Lord God made all sorts of trees grow up from the ground—trees that were beautiful and that produced delicious fruit. **(Genesis 2:8-9)**

We can therefore classify creation documented in Genesis 1:1-25 as assets given to man and that an asset is anything that has value. Value increases where there is no competitor to provide an alternative. God's creation was priceless, and once given to man increased his net worth tremendously.

The Lord God placed the man in the Garden of Eden to tend and watch over it. **(Genesis 2:15)**

Net worth is the total value of the assets a person or corporation owns; minus the liabilities owed. Since Adam was a beneficiary of a fully funded state benefit, he incurred no debts and had zero liabilities. According to scripture, Adam's needs were covered solely by God; he lived in a fully maintained garden and could eat anything besides the fruit from the Tree of Good and Evil.

... You may freely eat the fruit of every tree in the garden.

(Genesis 2:6a)

The original man had no liabilities; any liability would significantly decline his value and power. Man remaining compliant with God's contractual agreement ensured his needs were satisfied with no personal expense; if he lived faithful to God, he would continue to enjoy the luxuries of Eden. Since a contract is a legally binding agreement between two or more persons or entities, God created and initiated the deal; he also defined the terms of the contract in Genesis 2: 16-17:

But the Lord God warned him, "You may freely eat the fruit of every tree in the garden— except the tree of the knowledge of good and evil. If you eat its fruit, you are sure to die."

A thorough analysis of the scriptures shows that man's value, worth, and power declined significantly after the fall. Sin meant man could no longer live free of cost in Eden.

So, the Lord God banished them from the Garden of Eden, and he sent Adam out to cultivate the ground from which he had been made. ***(Genesis 3:23)***

Work is not a consequence of sin since work was given before the fall. Before the fall, time was exchanged for value. Adam had full stewardship over God's possession; all his needs were catered for because of the value. Now in Genesis 3:23, God introduced a new type of work that required him to exchange effort for time.

There is no Biblical account in which God allowed Adam to carry any of the assets he once enjoyed from the Garden of Eden. Consequently, a new arrangement was set up in which time was now traded for effort. Effort guarantees food and other necessities. No effort, no satisfaction of needs.

By the sweat of your brow will you have food to eat until you return to the ground from which you were made.

(Genesis 3:19)

If wealth is the abundance of valuable possessions and money, we can infer that Adam's choice to dishonour God affected him spiritually and financially. He had no assets, therefore, no wealth. Adam's nine to five was woefully inadequate to guarantee wealth acquisition. Wealth and fulfilment simultaneously are directly tied to our obedience to God, His Word, and His Will. In Genesis 26, we meet another man whose choice to honour God transformed his finances, empowered him, and allowed him to possess assets. Scripture teaches that it was the most severe famine, and Isaac was tempted to go to Egypt.

A severe famine now struck the land, as had happened before in Abraham's time. So, Isaac moved to Gerar, where Abimelech, king of the Philistines, lived. The Lord appeared to Isaac and said, "Do not go down to Egypt, but do as I tell you. Live here as a foreigner in this land, and I will be with you and bless you. I hereby confirm that I will give all these lands to you and your descendants, just as I solemnly promised Abraham, your father. I will cause your descendants to become as numerous as the stars of the sky, and I will give them all these lands. And through your descendants all the nations of the earth will be blessed. I will do this because Abraham listened to me and obeyed all my requirements, commands, decrees, and instructions." So, Isaac stayed in Gerar. **(Genesis 26)**

Even with the most significant financial crisis, financial freedom begins with obeying God and His Word. Poverty is not an excuse to dishonour God. Isaac obeyed God and generated assets despite being one of the most challenging times. Difficulty does not deter investment. Investing is the act of allocating resources with the hope of generating an income or profit. Investment requires careful market analysis, examining what is lacking to create a solution capable of yielding high returns. Hardships are not the reason to quit but to make a conscious assessment and prayerfully produce a product that the world will purchase regardless of the value. Where demand increases and supplies weaken value increases. This is called value appreciation. Isaac diversified his portfolio by planting crops and rearing varying animals. This earned him a significant return, raising his influence and yielding financial freedom.

When Isaac planted his crops that year, he harvested a hundred times more grain than he planted, for the Lord blessed him. He became a very rich man, and his wealth continued to grow. He acquired so many flocks of sheep and goats, herds of cattle, and servants that the Philistines became jealous of him.

(Genesis 26:14)

As the value increases, the man must take steps to reduce any debts. Acquiring debts is equivalent to being in bondage.

Just as the rich rule the poor, so the borrower is a servant to the lender. ***(Proverbs 22:7)***

Not only does debt enslave you, but it binds your entire family or household. In the Bible, we learn of a widow who came crying to the prophet for assistance because her son was about to be entered into slavery because of the outstanding debts of her late husband.

One day the widow of a member of the group of prophets came to Elisha and cried out, "My husband who served you is dead, and you know how he feared the Lord. But now a creditor has come, threatening to take my two sons as slaves." **(1 Kings 4:1)**

The responsible man works hard, saves as much as possible, and secures health and life insurance to eliminate bringing his family into insurmountable debts.

Finally, cultivate and practice good spending habits. These include:

Create a budget. The development and maintenance of a budget correspond to a 'future plan' for spending money. It is a valuable tool for managing money. Budgeting helps the man to gain a good overview of his financial obligations and provides a guide for their fulfilment.

Managing cash flow. Cash flow is the net amount of cash and cash equivalents being transferred into and out of your account. Managing cash flow requires the man to control his income and expenditure reasonably. To accomplish this, he must frequently assess his financial standing and apply strict disciplinary measures to ensure he is always financially sound. As he manages his cash flow, he must remain aware that cash devalues over time owing to inflation and other factors, while assets appreciate with time. He must, therefore, actively seek opportunities to raise his income. This may be done through investing in REITs, stocks, and bonds. The goal is to earn more while spending less. As you increase in assets, use the profit acquired to purchase your needs. Every man should position himself to supply the essentials for his family, namely house, transportation, food, education, healthcare, utility, and clothing.

To gain a more detailed insight into achieving financial success, please register for our life-changing course entitled "**Critical Keys for Financial Freedom**." This course is designed with you in mind and is intended to give you essential, step-by-step practical, workable, and Biblical keys to raising your income, increasing your value, providing tips for wealth creation, and managing your debt and cash flow. Also, purchase our book "**Critical Keys for Financial Freedom**." Details for accessing our courses and books can be obtained at the rear of this book.

Affirmations:

- I will demonstrate proper stewardship regarding my financial affairs. I affirm that God is the owner of all things, and I am manager.

- I am committed to debt reduction, management, and ultimate freedom. I will submit myself to sound financial instructions and practice.

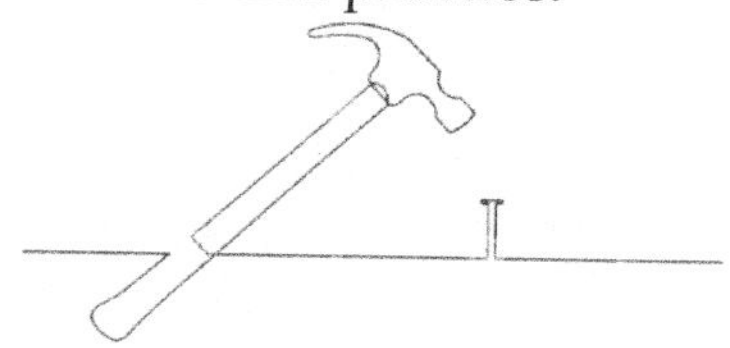

MAN, AND HIS SEXUALITY

Sexuality is one of the biggest parts of who we are.

<u>*Carla Gugino*</u>

Sexuality is perhaps the most delicate topic for men, especially in Western Culture. His sexuality makes him feel powerful. Sexuality is the capacity to possess sexual feelings and, likewise, to engage in the act. God originally designed sexuality to distinguish between maleness and femaleness, which is the primary key to gender identity and distinction. The expressions of sexuality are, therefore, deeply rooted and founded in God's overall design for man. The height of sexual expression is demonstrated in a heterosexual union established by God. For a woman, sex is for pleasure, the need to feel loved, while for a man, it's an occasion to affirm power, guaranteeing fulfilment. God creates sexual intercourse to fulfil the needs of both man and woman.

What Do Women Need?

Women needs to be loved and cherished.

For husbands, this means love your wives, just as Christ loved the church. He gave up his life for her to make her holy and clean, washed by the cleansing of God's word. He did this to present her to himself as a glorious church without a spot or wrinkle or any other blemish. Instead, she will be holy and without fault. In the same way, husband's ought to love their wives as they love their own bodies. For a man who loves his wife shows love for himself. No one hates his own body but feeds and cares for it, just as Christ cares for the church. And we are members of his body. ***(Ephesians 5:25-30)***

Since the scripture emphasises the need for the woman to be loved, we can infer that she possesses a void that can only be filled with her husband's love. We may also insinuate that the all-knowing God, the creator of sex, would create sexual intercourse bearing the woman's needs in mind. It is not the only way for her to experience love, but it is undoubtedly one medium through which she identifies her true self and feels fulfilled. Where there is a lack or limitation of sexual intercourse, a woman may feel unloved, ugly, unwanted, or worthless. Good sex indicates that her husband loves her and craves to be with her only and always. According to research conducted by Canadian researchers in 2012, as cited in Dean (2020), the part of your brain that handles emotions is where sexual desire comes from. Therefore, both emotional love and sexual desire are from the insular cortex. These findings underscore the interconnectivity between love and sex, almost removing our will to choose. We can choose to have sex when love is absent, but it can be difficult for emotions to handle. Another research by Penn State researchers suggests that most women surveyed believed that when love is present, the sexual experience is better and more fulfilling. Therefore, sex satisfies an essential need for the woman. Men should frequently seek to provide this well-needed service to build their wives' confidence, assurance of love, and commitment to relationships. The husband should fulfil his wife's sexual needs, likewise the wife should fulfil her husband's needs.

The master plan of God's enemy, satan, is to simultaneously encourage man to engage in and enjoy a lot of sex outside of marriage and discourage its frequency in marriage.

Declarations:

- I will not be trapped in sex outside of a marital covenant.
- I will enjoy sex within the covenant of my marriage.

What Do Men Need?

Clear communication, respect, and honesty are critical for men. It helps them to open and reveal their innermost desires and insecurities. Men want to be understood, loved, and appreciated. Paying attention to their unspoken words (cues) and giving them personal space is vital for strengthening the relationship and encouraging further communication. They want to be affirmed frequently and cherished unconditionally. Men want to be their wife's priority and not their afterthought.

Wives, submit yourselves unto your own husbands, as unto the Lord. For the husband is the head of the wife, even as Christ is the head of the church: and he is the saviour of the body. Therefore, as the church is subject unto Christ, so let the wives be to their own husbands in everything. **(Ephesians 5:22-23)**

'Submit' carries the idea of accepting or yielding to another person's superior force, authority, or will. There is an inner part that wants to feel relevant, and the willing submission of his wife achieves this. Therefore, we can infer that the all-knowing God designed sex as a resourceful mechanism to enable the wife to surrender her reigns to her powerful husband allowing him to conquer her most intimate needs. Good sex may impact how a man perceives himself. It makes him feel respected, honoured, loved, and appreciated—this feeling of power, uniqueness, and desire propels him to serve his purpose.

An empowered man will go around feeling like a general manager all day. When the man lacks confidence in his potency and ability to satisfy his wife, he may become withdrawn, jealous, and often depressed, and void sexual encounters. His sexuality identifies with his manhood. No man wants to know his wife is unsatisfied. Any thought of her dissatisfaction may affect him physically, psychologically, emotionally, socially, spiritually, and financially.

The difference in needs becomes obvious in how they (man and woman) express their fulfilment through conversations with peers. A woman may say, "I feel so loved. He was so sweet, and I enjoyed every moment of the sexual encounter. I love him." The same man sharing with his friend may say, "Brethren, last night I was awesome; I did very well; her reaction was phenomenal; I made her orgasm."

What is different in the expressions is one is about the feeling desired, and the other is about performance.

What Sexual Exploits Are Out of Bounds?

It is widely embraced, especially among some religious communities, that a man is free to engage in whatsoever sexual exploits he deems appropriate once legally married. Scripture must guide man's action in and out of the bedroom.

Marriage is honourable in all, and the bed undefiled: but whoremongers and adulterers God will judge. **(Hebrews 13:4)**

This text aims not to define or create a list of actions or apparatus that are acceptable for marriage; however, we will attempt to correct the inappropriate application of this text about man honouring through his sexuality.

Let us examine one of the critical words in this text: 'honourable' is derived from the Greek word 'timios', meaning valuable, costly, or precious. The author of the scripture pushed back at the normalisation of the sexually immoral culture embraced by the people at that time, reminding them that marriage between a man and a woman is precious, valuable, and costly. As such, one should regard it as special and worthy of being cherished.

The beautiful design for marriage is often dishonoured through the following:

- Common law and visiting unions resulting in the participation of sexual relations outside of marriage.
- Adultery that is having sex with someone else outside of your partner. (We define marriage as a union between one man and one woman).
- Neglecting each other.
- Any attempt to redefine marriage.
- Divorce or any other form of separation justified or unjustified.

Disclaimer: Divorce is a very controversial topic, with people holding several views. Our attempt in this book is not to teach the wrongness or rightness of divorce but to establish what we perceive in scripture as God's ideal. He would prefer if a man would marry a woman, and both would remain faithful to each other throughout their lifetime.

The scriptures clearly state, *"A man leaves his father and mother and is joined to his wife, and the two are united into one."* **(Genesis 2:24)**

Anything that alters or destroys the tenets of God's original plan for marriage devalues it. Therefore, the value of marriage can only be maintained or appreciated when practiced in sync with God's idea of marriage. The text further states that the bed is undefiled, which is usually interpreted as marriage is a sovereign state that allows couples to establish and live by any standard that brings them pleasure or satisfaction. In our quest for pleasure, we must remember that marriage falls within God's rule, and while you have been given certain rights to each other's body, you are still required to conform to God's standard. Ancient Israel was deemed honourable but was not allowed to adopt and practice the culture of the heathen. It is dangerous to base your sexuality on and define pleasure based on the worldly culture we reside in.

As you seek to honour God with your sexuality consider the following:

- Who or what is influencing your sexuality?
- Where do your ideas for pleasure derive? Who are you patterning?
- What does the Bible teach about those practices? Does this glorify God?

Our sexuality should honour God first; He is glorified when we treat our spouses well. Ensure your spouse feels loved, appreciated, respected, desired, cherished, valued, and beautiful. Do your practices reduce your spouse to a thing, a machine, or a toy you use when you are bored or for your selfish gratification? The scripture teaches about two men who built their houses, one on a rock and the other on the sand. Both structures were completed, and both builders were hardworking; the only difference was where the building was constructed. In the text, the man described as foolish built his house on the sand (foundation). In this book, we will define the sand as the views of our friends, society, porn movies, and other influential societal elements. How many of you are unhappy with your spouse's performance in bed because of an expectation you derived from a movie you watched or a conversation you had? God is interested in your sexuality and created it for you to enjoy. Have you engaged him recently in a discussion concerning those needs you have?

And this same God who takes care of me will supply all your needs from his glorious riches, which have been given to us in Christ Jesus. **(Philippians 4:19)**

The scripture describes the other man as wise because he built his house on the rock. For this book, we will describe the rock as God, His ways, His will, and His word. Are your thoughts being influenced by God? We have enough examples in scripture to have a beautiful and fulfilled sexuality.

The king is lying on his couch, enchanted by the fragrance of my perfume. My lover is like a sachet of myrrh, lying between my breasts. He is like a bouquet of sweet henna blossoms from the vineyards of En-gedi. How beautiful you are, my darling, how beautiful! Your eyes are like doves. You are so handsome, my love, pleasing beyond words! The soft grass is our bed fragrant cedar branches are the beams of our house, and pleasant-smelling firs are the rafters. ***(Songs of Solomon 1:12-17)***

Our sexuality is beautiful and should be thoroughly enjoyed but within the parameters of God's expectation. The New Living Translation gives a more compound explanation of the beauty of sex within marriage.

Give honour to marriage and remain faithful to one another in marriage. God will surely judge people who are immoral and those who commit adultery. ***(Hebrews 13:4)***

To gain a more detailed insight into maximising your sexual ambitions, please register for our life-changing course entitled **"Critical Keys for Developing Sexual**

Intimacy in Marriage." This course is designed with you in mind and is intended to give you essential, step-by-step practical, workable, and Biblical for greater and more productive sexual exploits in marriage. Also, purchase our book "**21 Shades: A Practical Guide to Growing Intimacy in Marriage**."

Affirmations:

- I recognise that scripturally there are fundamental differences with what constitutes maleness and femaleness.
- I agree that the expressions of sexual intimacy are reserved for marriage unions.
- I affirm as the creator did that marriage is between a man and women in a lifelong covenantal relationship.

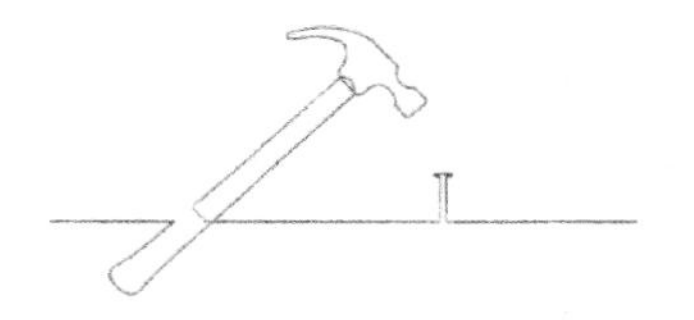

MAN, AND HIS INTEGRITY

Live so that when your children think of fairness, caring, and integrity, they think of you.

H. Jackson Brown, Jr.

At the heart of every man is the will to be honest, upright, sincere, truthful, and trustworthy. Using data gathered from observation and interaction, we conclude that even those regarded as menaces to society have a desire for their family to live and enjoy peace and tranquillity. A recent newspaper report showed that the 'dons' (those who lead criminal organisations) seek the best education for their children in the most prestigious institutions. They do not want their children to pattern their lifestyles and embrace qualities foreign to integrity. The police held a young man wanted for killing at least thirteen people recently. He desperately pleaded with his captives to spare his life, as he wanted better for his family. He exclaimed he did not want this same life for his children. How could a renowned criminal cry for mercy?

He could because he was wired to be like His creator, God. God has integrity, and so does man.

"Let us make human beings in our image, to be like us.

(Genesis 1:26)

Within his set up, he was created to possess the qualities of God. Even though he lives outside God's expectations, he knows his acts are unacceptable. Amidst the category you identify with, such as atheist, agnostic, unbeliever, Muslim, Hindu, or non-religious, you are fitted with a moral compass that makes you feel guilty when you practice immorality. Regardless of our religious, political, or personal persuasion, we all accept certain qualities to be humane, such as honesty, truthfulness, and trust. There is only one possible explanation: we were all created to have His maker's qualities. Therefore, whatever displeases God affects us. We experience joy and fulfilment when we practice godliness. We can therefore infer that guilt is a trigger that alerts us when we have participated or are actively engaged in practices outside God's nature. Integrity supersedes religion; it is the characteristics we possess that connect us to God.

Let us examine what the Bible teaches about integrity:

The godly walk with integrity; blessed are their children who follow them. **(Proverbs 20:7)**

The term' integrity' derives from the Hebrew word 'tome,'' meaning 'the condition of being without blemish, completeness, perfection, sincerity, soundness, uprightness, and wholeness.' God requires us, as men, to walk upright and blameless. One may argue, 'I can't be perfect.' That is partially true: The idea of perfection does not imply 'sinless perfection''. Note what John writes:

My dear children, I am writing this to you so that you will not sin. But if anyone does sin, we have an advocate who pleads our case before the father. He is Jesus Christ, the one who is truly righteous. ***(1 John 2:1)***

John stated what would be the ideal, a sinless state; however, he sought to encourage believers that despite their errors, they can be whole, complete, or perfect because Jesus is their defence attorney. Therefore, we are made perfect through our exclusive submission and obedience to God's Word. The man of integrity must rely on God wholly and solely. Another may frown upon the thought of ever reaching a state of absolute blamelessness. Let us examine what Jesus taught in the Sermon on the Mount.

God blesses you when people mock you and persecute you and lie about you and say all sorts of evil things against you because you are my followers. 12 Be happy about it! Be very glad! For a great reward awaits you in heaven. And remember, the ancient prophets were persecuted in the same way. ***(Matthew 5:11-12)***

The issue is not 'being blamed' we must ensure that whatever we are accused of that is immoral is false. We must not allow the following to be named among us: dishonesty, stealing, envy, adultery, unfaithfulness, covetousness.

Sexual immorality, impurity, lustful pleasures, idolatry, sorcery, hostility, quarrelling, jealousy, outbursts of anger, selfish ambition, dissension, division, envy, drunkenness, wild parties, and other sins like these. ***(Galatians 5:19-21)***

Integrity means 'honesty and adherence to a pattern of good works.' Our excellent work considers all our interpersonal and interrelation connections, such as the promises we make. When you are a man of integrity, your word should be your bond. Do not promise what you cannot provide, and where you have made pledges do your best to honour them to a high standard. In unusual circumstances where you cannot honour an undertaking, take responsibility, provide a suitable apology, and find ways to make up for the inconvenience caused. This approach will tell people you are loyal, responsible, faithful, and trustworthy.

In everything, set them an example by doing what is good. In your teaching show integrity, seriousness and soundness of speech that cannot be condemned, so that those who oppose you may be ashamed because they have nothing bad to say about us. Jesus is our model of integrity. He demonstrated that integrity is doing the right thing every time. Discomfort or challenges is not an excuse to forfeit integrity. Jesus had just completed his forty days of fasting in the wilderness when Satan approached him.

During that time, the devil came and said to him, "If you are the Son of God, tell these stones to become loaves of bread."

(Matthew 4:3)

Your integrity will be tested when you are most vulnerable. He was hungry and could do well with a meal of bread, but still, He chose to remain loyal to His father. In our capacities as ministers, we have heard many provide feeble excuses for acts of immorality. For example, she no longer makes me happy, so I cheated. True integrity is when we can do the right thing, even when we experience hurt and disappointment. There is no time off from integrity, and there is no excuse good enough to justify our failure to exemplify Christ. Notice that the enemy challenged Christ "if thou be the Son of God." Many fail simply at trying to prove worth and value. Integrity is steadfastness in our walk with Christ, seeking only to please Christ.

Another observation is that Jesus was wholly man, not just God suggesting that there was an aspect of Him that could desire to do evil and therefore needed to be grounded and disciplined to fulfil His father and His will. Quite often in scripture, He reiterated, "not my Will but thy will be done." This could perhaps explain the need for this and other regular moments of prayer.

For we have not a high priest which cannot be touched with the feeling of our infirmities; but was in all points tempted like as we are, yet without sin. **(Hebrews 4:15)**

We must strive to do the right thing every time.

Let us pray:

Dear Lord,
Help me to always pursue righteousness and to be responsible with choices I make Lord reveal my errors so I can correct them. Amen.

...Be an example to all believers in what you say, in the way you live, in your love, your faith, and your purity. **(1 Timothy 4:12)**

Affirmations:

- I promise to be transparent and open in all my dealings and undertakings.
- I will avoid being deceptive. I affirm that my word is my bond.

- I will honour God through my marriage by loving, cherishing, nourishing, sacrificing, and honouring my partner.

- I will continually pray with and for my wife to demonstrate both my commitment to her and God.

- I will not give the enemy any occasion to destroy my marriage.

- I realise that my obligation to pray will not just be self but other focused.

- I will allow the principles of God's word to lead me and not the rules and assumptions I learn from the world.

- I will uphold the standards of truth and fair play.

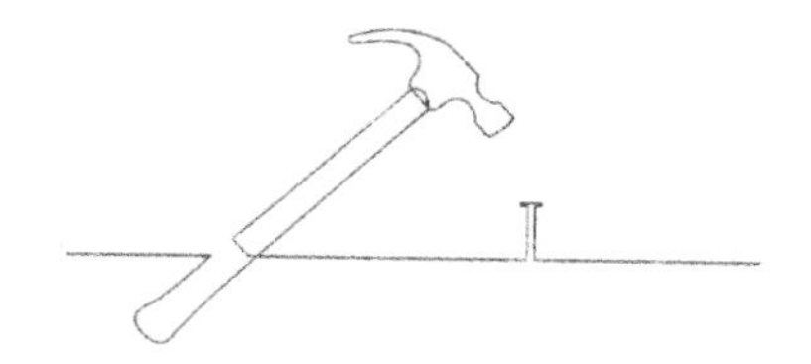

MAN, AND HIS MENTALITY

I learned that one's mentality can influence how they react to physical obstacles.

Lee Seung-gi

Man was God's first human capital in the world. God made a significant investment when He carefully designed man in His image and likeness and breathed life into man.

He became a living soul. ***(Genesis 2:7)***

When we examine the scripture through a psycho-spiritual lens, we will realise man only became a living soul possessing a mind after God deposited His breath into him. According to the APA dictionary, the soul is "the nonphysical aspect of a human being, considered responsible for the functions of the mind and individual personality and often thought to live on after the death of the physical body." The English word corresponds to the Greek 'psyche', often translated as 'mind,' and the Latin 'anima', usually translated as 'spirit.' A man who is disconnected from God is just a body walking around mindless, lacking the ability to reason logically. Such a man lives short of his purpose since purpose can only be realised when he shares an intimate relationship with the creator. An example of a man mentally, psychologically, physically, and spiritually disconnected from God and his fellow men is recorded in Luke 15. This man made several poor decisions that negatively affected him and those who loved him the most, including his father. An unstable mind affects everyone. Restoration begins with a change of mind. It was not until he became conscious of his subconscious state that he realised how much he lived beneath his purpose.

When he finally came to his senses, he said to himself, 'At home even the hired servants have food enough to spare, and here I am dying of hunger! **(Luke 15:17)**

Right decisions are the product of a stable mind (one connected to God).

The man lay lifeless, unable to think, interact or engage with the world around him until God breathed into his nostrils. God's breath generated his personality and shaped his identity. The human soul is central to the personhood of a human being. God made man a 'living soul,' allowing him to unlock all the mysteries of the wonderful world He created, that is, to problem-solve, rationalise, and deduce. George MacDonald said, "You don't have a soul. You are a Soul, and you have a body."

The breath of God, the life and power of God, given to man animated him. He became curious, assessed, and made decisions, the most detrimental being exploring what God forbade, resulting in the initial transgression that would affect all his successors.

Poor decisions affect all; the only cure is a mind stayed on Christ.

Don't copy the behaviour and customs of this world, but let God transform you into a new person by changing the way you think. Then you will learn to know God's will for you, which is good and pleasing and perfect. **(Romans 12:2)**

Consequently, satan, the enemy of our souls, our fallen nature, and the world reprogram our mentality, training us to subscribe to our free will instead of God's directives, essentially disobeying God's expectation. Only a man in his right mind can please God. This act of disobedience is called 'Thinking error' in Psychology. Since the incident in Eden, man's mind continues to be influenced by the ideologies of the devil, the world, and his falling nature, leading to ill actions, fears, and disappointment. We have the predisposition to live beneath God's standards, often resulting in anxiety, depression, manipulation, and other various forms of disorders and discomforts. Consequently, several men have lost their sense of direction. To free ourselves from the cognitive errors implanted through sin, we must connect with God. A restored relationship with our maker means an alignment to His vision.

You must have the same attitude that Christ Jesus had.

(Philippians 2:5)

We can only become 'mind pure' when we seek to inhibit the mind of God through reading His word and frequently dialoguing with Him through prayer. 'As we seek God, we die to 'self,' and our soul reconnects to its source, God. Our greatest potential can be found in Christ (Colossians 3:3). Why? Because God made us, like any manufacturer, He knows the intent and capacity of our minds. He gave us all a measure of faith, showing that we all have the power to reason, think, and believe. Your ability to believe must start with the 'mind.' As men, we must manage our minds daily, subjected to daily mind renewal by partnering with God. Only God knows what you can accomplish on earth. Freely choose His will.

How Choice Informs Our Mentality.

The ability to choose affects man's thinking. Our actions are often based on how we feel in the moment. It is an impulsive reaction to unfavourable experiences. We must consult God to aid in the process of restoration. Progress demands redirection.

"It is hardly possible to build anything if frustration, bitterness, and a mood of helplessness prevail." —Lech Walesa

Before the advent of sin man's predisposition to decision making was to engage in sincere consultation with God regarding every matter. He was clear that success could only be obtained through consistent partnership with God.

Study this Book of Instruction continually. Meditate on it day and night so you will be sure to obey everything written in it. Only then will you prosper and succeed in all you do.

(Joshua 1:8)

Our unwillingness to submit to God's will is affected by the two main structures within the human mind, the conscious and the unconscious. According to Freudian theory, the conscious mind includes everything we know or can quickly recall and is responsible for directing our attention and perceive events that we need to respond to in our immediate environment. These includes fantasies, feelings, memories, perceptions, self-awareness, sensations, and thoughts. Essentially it is anything we can think about. Often our memories about past hurt, thoughts about future struggles and the effect of the current pain affects our decisions and ultimately our way of life. This can lead to us feeling fearful, lonely, and depressed. Our response must be faith in God and His promises. The Scriptures are replete with His promises. With each promise, God vows that something will (or will not) happen or be given or come to pass. These are not frivolous or casual pledges like we often make. They are rock-solid, unequivocal commitments made by God Himself and are irreversible and unstoppable. God is faithful and therefore, we the believers can have complete assurance that His promises will be realised.

On the other hand, the unconscious mind includes everything outside of our understanding, our hopes, wishes, desires, urges, and memories that resides outside of our awareness and control. They possess the proclivity to influence our conduct.

What must be our response? Faith in God.

Let us hold tightly without wavering to the hope we affirm, for God can be trusted to keep his promise. ***(Hebrews 10:23)***

As humans, God reserves some things from us, within the secret cabinet of our unconscious mind; we don't know everything. Only God is Omniscient; He is the repository of all knowledge. We cannot have wisdom outside of God, so we must talk to Him frequently and fervently.

If you need wisdom, ask our generous God, and he will give it to you. He will not rebuke you for asking. **(James 1:5)**

We often make poor decisions and get into unwanted problems because we do not surrender our entire being including our minds to God. Consciously submit today for a more productive tomorrow. Every meaningful change begins with the mind.

Affirmations:

- I promise to perform optimally in all my endeavours.
- I will be faithful as a steward with what God has invested within me to ensure significant returns that will be for his honour and Glory.

- I will fulfil the purpose for which I was created in my Generation.

- I will never allow my ego to consume my thinking and deject emotional reasoning.

- I will not allow my life to be characterised by sin instead I will be obedient to God.

- I will honour my marriage covenant through being faithful to my partner.

- I will preserve my sexual purity and only engage in the sanctity of marriage.

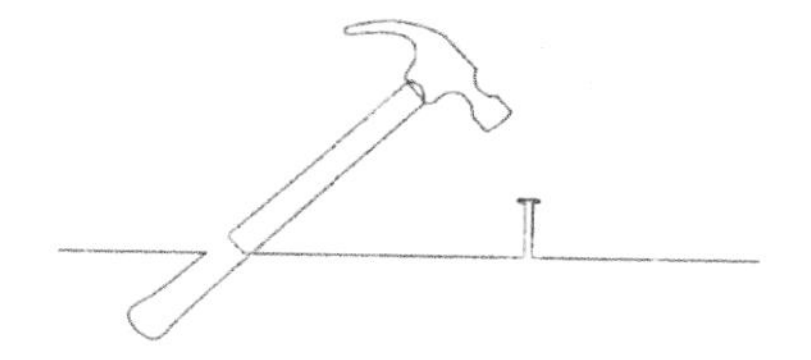

MAN, AND HIS ANOTOMY OF THINKING

"Our happiness depends on the habit of mind we cultivate."

<u>Norman Vincent Peale</u>

According to Freud, the unconscious mind helps shape our personality and creates three significant components: ID, Ego, and superego.

- **The ID:**

  The 'ID' is the deepest part of our mind locked away in the unconscious compartment, creating a desire for ongoing pleasure. We believe ID led Adam and Eve to eat the fruit God forbid, in pursuit of pleasure. Man always seeks pleasure, which often push him further away from God and His will.

- **The Ego:**

  The ego shapes who we become. Contrary to popular belief, the ego is the objective aspect of our mind, balancing pleasure, and morality, allowing man to interact with society and its norms.

- **The Superego:**

  This aspect of the mind determines who we become. It carries the data of God's original plan for man and stores the morals, values, and principles our parents, family, and society taught us. The superego tries to get the ID to conform to a standard of Godliness. Still, because the ID is locked away in the unconscious, it often does not conform to what is morally and spiritually acceptable. Man's mentality is constantly at war because of the different views these three components of the mind present daily. However, God's original plan for man was to conform to His will, not to live confused by the world's mentality. The challenge we face as men when we are disconnected from the mind of God, is colossal because we allow the world to socialise us and define how we see ourselves. A school of thought suggest we become who we are by nature, meaning the information we acquire through genes and the environment we are grown in determine our mentality. Many of us have inherited generational ideologies of what it means to be a man. This inherited information is stored in the filing cabinet in our unconscious mind, and they inform our daily thinking habits, impacting how we feel and behave. Almost all men have what appears to be a strong fighting spirit. Through years of hard-wired information, we learn that real men are strong, tough, and do not cry. This prevents us from being emotionally vulnerable to deal effectively with life's challenges and seek professional help. This kind of thinking is unhelpful and usually results in mental health challenges, anger, and other maladaptive behaviours. When distorted thinking influences how

IOBI

we see ourselves, the world, and people, we become unclear of our purpose while losing our original identity, leading to mental, physical, and spiritual confusion.

Identity vs. Role confusion.

According to research, one of the most frequently asked questions by men is Who Am I? We all want to feel a sense of belonging. Our minds make us curious and propel us to search for answers, often it is unable to supply the desired information therefore we must pursue God, our manufacturer. Only God can supply the wisdom we need. Paul encourages us to resist the urge to conform to this world but to be transformed by renewing the mind (Romans 12:2). Failing to renew our minds in God and conform to His instructions often leads to identity crisis which has the propensity to be consequential. No one succeeds without first knowing who they are.

The psychosocial view of Psychology postulates "if the man fails to uncover his identity at an early age, by the time he becomes a teenager, he will experience a crisis of identity giving rise to the combative struggle between identity and role confusion. This in turn determines the type of adult the individual become. End this war on truth within the mind today by subscribing to a relentless faith in God. You are who God says you are, a man made to lead and love your family. You are a good example of morality. <u>YOUR GENDER </u>is a male.

We must seek to understand who we are as men. Failing to discover God's original intention for our life will lead to a stage where we are unsure of:

- who we are.
- whose we are.

Several persons, in particular men have lost their sense of self and ultimately their purpose. Society's ideologies and culture has distorted their way of thinking, which has serious consequences for their purpose, relationships, family, and personal fulfilment. Every man, including who are trapped in illicit behaviour, promiscuity, and affected by mental illness is valuable. He can return to his manufacturer, God, and have his mind renewed. God can redeem anyone from confusion, resetting their mentality to live as a benefactor of renewed hope. Overcoming 'role confusion,' requires one to conquer the dysfunctional rules and assumptions about what it means to be a man.

Impact of unhelpful Rules and Assumptions on Mentality.

When God made us, He designed us for His purpose. The consequence of living based on our will leads to the blatant disregard for Biblical principles in pursuit of our perceptions and feelings. This has led many of us into a 'rabbit hole' of negative automatic thoughts. These thoughts suddenly appear in our minds, driven by our innate desire to err, the devil, and the world, affecting our behaviours. In Psychology, we call it Negative Automatic Thoughts, rules, and assumptions we gather throughout our life and store in our unconscious minds. John warns us to.

Love not the world, neither the things that are in the world. If any man loves the world, the love of the Father is not in him.

(1 John 2:15)

When life gets tough, we often struggle to cope because we are unclear of God's will. Such experiences force us to rely on the data stored in our unconscious mind that is the unhelpful rules and assumptions that motivates our actions. These rules usually manifest as 'should and must' and 'If then' thinking, e.g., "I should be at a better place in my life, I am worthless" If I am not working, then that means I am a failure." These unhelpful rules cause men to engage in black-and-white thinking, in which they fail to see God as the grey area who can supply all their needs no matter what stage they are in life. When we cannot meet the unrealistic standards, we set for ourselves and the traditions laid out by society, we will likely become isolated and closed. This further intensifies unhelpful thinking and results in rumination and worry. We must seek to restore hope and faith in God. We must pursue a closer relation with God to ensure we live in conjunction with His intent for our identity and not that of the world.

We must manage our minds becoming that living soul daily, that is connected to God fully. If we do this, we will not lean on our understanding, which will surely fail us. Society or its expectation for our lives should not define the way we think nor our conduct; we should develop our mentality grounded in the principles of God.

We can make our plans, but the Lord determines our steps.

(Proverbs 16:9)

Affirmations:

- I will allow the knowledge of God to control my cognitive ability and not to allow negative thoughts to determine my mood and behaviour.

- I will never allow the perception generated from the world to deceive me into living in denial and senseless captivity. I will scrutinise all my thoughts because they are not facts.

- I will dedicate myself to the construction of a firm, spiritual and mental muscle so I can fulfil purpose. I recognise that as a leader I am always accountable to God who will ultimately evaluate my stewardship.

- I will embrace and commit to lead in all spheres of society and seek to engage others in the process.

- I will not shirk from my responsibility but will exercise authority in all my spheres of leadership not as a Lord but as Servant (Steward). I will lead in such a way that order replaces chaos.

- I will not shirk from my responsibility but will exercise authority in all my spheres of leadership not as a Lord but as Servant (Steward).

- I will lead in such a way that order replaces chaos. I promise to unconditionally love and honour my spouse.

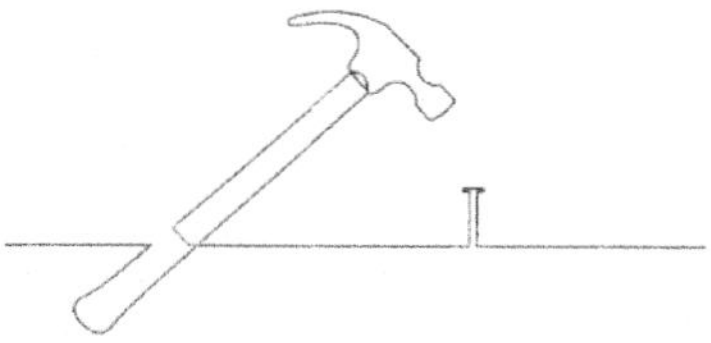

MAN, AND HIS VOICE

"Words mean more than what is set down on paper. It takes a man voice to infuse them with deeper meaning".

Maya Angelou

One of the most vivid childhood memories we share of our father was his ability to walk into a room and command order without uttering a single word. His presence was the voice inspired, shivering among rude boys while prompting them to fall in line. We had an inbuilt ability to decrypt his facial expression and execute his intent as expected. Dad was like an emergency tool that mom referenced "behold the night cometh when your father shall return." That statement was like a code capable of transforming naughty boys to saint-like kids. Dad did not speak much, but when he did, it carried meaningful and effective signals igniting changes and commanding order. It was that he was not cruel and boisterous but an authoritative voice. You simply conformed to his directives when he spoke. When God constructed man, he created him to possess Godly qualities. One such quality is the ability to speak things forth, which should happen when a man speaks.

Let us make human beings in our image, to be like us.

(Genesis 1:26)

In Genesis, the Bible teaches us that God spoke everything into existence; that is, the sun, moon, waters, plants, animals, and birds all came into existence from the mere utterance of God. This sharply describes the power, authority, and sovereignty of God. Before creation, there was no order or what is described as chaos within theological circles, but God spoke six days, continuously ordering and organizing the universe we have today. The seas, oceans, land, trees, and creatures all came into order at the sound of God's instruction. If man was created in

God's nature, he is meant to command order and inspire changes through his voice.

Let us examine the scripture for some men who inspired changes through speaking:

Adam was tasked to name all living creatures; in essence, whatever he spoke became the order of the day.

He brought them to the man to see what he would call them, and the man chose a name for each one. He gave names to all the livestock, all the birds of the sky, and all the wild animals. But still there was no helper just right for him. ***(Genesis 2:19:20)***

We, too, have been given the power to name our children, streets, cities, companies, and churches. This is the accepted norm among several cultures; however, in most jurisdictions, the types of names are regulated, for example:

- A parent cannot give a child an offensive name.
- Two companies cannot have the same name.

This is in keeping with our view of morality as we believe that Adam being perfect and God-like, would have chosen names that represented the nature and quality of the creature.

In Exodus, God called a man called Moses to tell Pharaoh to release his people from bondage.

"Go back to Pharaoh," the LORD commanded Moses. "Tell him, 'This is what the LORD, the God of the Hebrews, says: Let my people go, so they can worship me." ***(Exodus 9:1)***

We must open our mouths and speak out against injustice, discrimination, classism, elitism, prejudice, and other practice that encourage the maltreatment of any other human being.

Speak up for those who cannot speak for themselves; ensure justice for those being crushed. Yes, speak up for the poor and helpless, and see that they get justice. ***(Proverbs 31:8-9)***

In the Gospel of Matthew, Jesus authorised the church to bind up diabolical plots, weapons, or assignments from hell while speaking life and releasing favour and blessing over our lives, households, churches, and nations.

Upon this rock I will build my church, and all the powers of hell will not conquer it. And I will give you the keys of the Kingdom of Heaven. Whatever you forbid on earth will be forbidden in heaven, and whatever you permit on earth will be permitted in heaven. ***(Matthew 16:18-19)***

The prophet Nathan spoke to David, challenging him to repent for committing adultery with Uriah's wife and the deception and ultimate arrangement of Uriah's death.

So, the Lord sent Nathan the prophet to tell David this story: "There were two men in a certain town. One was rich, and one was poor. The rich man owned a great many sheep and cattle. The poor man owned nothing but one little lamb he had bought. He raised that little lamb, and it grew up with his children. It ate from the man's own plate and drank from his cup. He cuddled it in his arms like a baby daughter. One day a guest arrived at the home of the rich man. But instead of killing an animal from his own flock or herd, he took the poor man's lamb and killed it and prepared it for his guest." David was furious. "As surely as the Lord lives," he vowed, "any man who would do such a thing deserves to die! He must repay four lambs to the poor man for the one he stole and for having no pity. "Then Nathan said to David, "You are that man! The Lord, the God of Israel, says: I anointed you king of Israel and saved you from the power of Saul. I gave you your master's house and his wives and the kingdoms of Israel and Judah. And if that had not been enough, I would have given you much, much more. Why, then, have you despised the word of the Lord and done this horrible deed? For you have murdered Uriah the Hittite with the sword of the Ammonites and stolen his wife. From this time on, your family will live by the sword because you have despised me by taking Uriah's wife to be your own. ***(2 Samuel 12: 1-10)***

We must hold all perpetrators, religious leaders, political leaders, community leaders, and other officials accountable while encouraging them to be good examples of morality. Similarly, to the incident in the text, sexual crimes are prevalent in our society today. A study conducted by UN Women UK published in June 2021 found that 97% of women in the UK aged 18-24 have been sexually harassed, with a further 96% not reporting those situations because of the belief that it would not change anything. According to the National Sexual Violence Resource Centre (NSVR), one in five women in the United States experienced completed or attempted rape during their lifetime. As part of our God-given responsibility, we must protect our women and empower our boys to become future protectors. Like Nathan, we must collectively speak out against violence from our varying platforms, inspiring change, and challenging others to do the same. We must never allow immorality to be normalised in our midst.

Injustice anywhere is injustice everywhere.

-Martin Luther King

Your frequent and firm voice on societal issues should provoke others to do well. Do not allow the thought of being alone or inferior to hinder or discourage you from speaking as God's oracle on earth. One persistent voice is enough to gain the attention of others and propel them to do otherwise. Speak up and speak out! To be given dominion implies you can influence. Be imaginative and find ways to inspire others to do good.

Let us think of ways to motivate one another to acts of love and good works. And let us not neglect our meeting together, as some people do, but encourage one another, especially now that the day of his return is drawing near. ***(Hebrews 10:24)***

Our voices are the vehicles through which changes are inspired and realised. Not only do we speak up and out, but we can use our voices to encourage and persuade our fellow man. Some of the most influential leaders in history were described as charismatic because of their ability to connect with people on a deep level. Such leaders were precious within organisations, especially when facing a crisis or struggling to move forward. One such leader was the American Baptist minister and activist Dr. Martin

Luther King Jr. He became the most visible and influential spokesperson and leader in the American civil rights movement in the 1950s. He was:

- A strong communicator
- Empathetic and relatable
- Confident
- Motivational
- Engaging and charming
- Optimistic

With those traits, he inspired and gained support for the black community in a time when racism and social injustice were prevalent. His charismatic leadership was crucial in the Montgomery Bus Boycott, which lasted 385 days. This was in response to the arrest of Rosa Parks, a black American woman who refused to sit in the back of the bus and was subsequently arrested based on racial segregation laws. The King-led massive protest lasted for more than a year and is credited for the Supreme Court's final ruling that segregation on public buses was unconstitutional. Today all ethnic groups are free to sit anywhere while traveling on public transportation because one man believed in better and was willing to speak up until change was realised. You are positioned within this earth currently to inspire change, transform hearts, and empower people.

"Only by speaking out can we create lasting change. And that change begins with coming out." -DaShanne Stoke

Reflection:

- How have you been using your voice.

Let us pray:

Dear Lord,
Thank you for equipping me with voice to speak out on behalf of others 'I realise that my voice has the capacity to change situations and inspire others. Help me to use it to bring glory to your name.
Amen.

Affirmations:

- I will treat others with respect and honour. I am committed to constant communion and communication with God.

- I will never seek to engage in fraudulent or corrupt activities.

- I will uphold the same standards of right both publicly and privately.

- I promise to never allow my emotions to cause me to be spiteful or indifferent to the needs of others.

- I will be known for my lifestyle of honesty. I will seek to enrich the lives of others by inculcating a proper system of values.

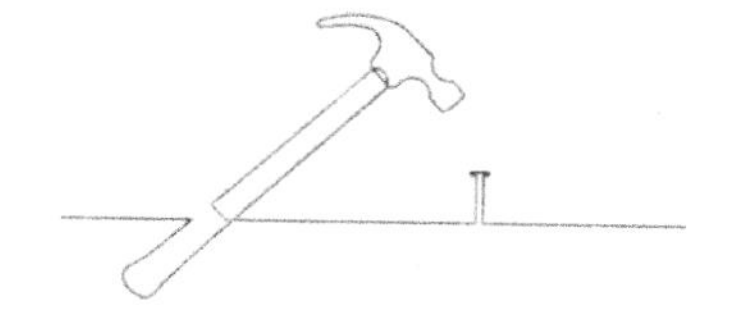

MAN, AND HIS WORTH

Thank you for making me so wonderfully complex! Your workmanship is marvellous—how well I know it.

<u>***Psalms 139:14***</u>

Man was deemed worthwhile from the creation; his qualities and esteem determine worth. Let us critically analysed Adam's worth:

- He was tailor made to meet the needs of the Garden.
- He was fitted with the characteristics of His maker.
- He was given authority over God's prestigious handiwork.
- He was entrusted with the right to name.

The best way to comprehend one's worth is to examine the value determined by its characteristics and the admiration others hold concerning the thing or person. I recall John, a middle-grade extraordinaire, sharing his understanding of value in his self-esteemed class. He posits that his understanding of value is rooted in the idea that others will do anything to be like you or to have what you have. This analysis was supported by two colloquial phrases often expressed by his father:

- A thief will not break into an empty house.
- A boy will not stone an empty tree.

Let us examine statement 1: *"A thief will not break into an empty house."*

The ultimate reason one risks his life and freedom to trespass on a property is its value, and the contents within the house are valuable, useful, and worth exchanging. Friend, you were carefully and meticulously constructed with purpose and given value that cannot be compared to any other living creature.

For in one place the scriptures say, "*What are mere mortals that you should think about them, or a son of man that you should care for him? Yet for a little while you made them a little lower than the angels and crowned them with glory and honour You gave.* **(Psalms 8:4-5)**

The worth of an individual is measured by his value and position within the hierarchy chain. Therefore, the higher one ascends along this prestigious ladder of upward mobility will positively impact his value and, ultimately, his worth. Adam was assigned as the top-ranking official on earth, having the right to rule over everything within this jurisdiction. Man's position in leadership gave him direct access to the creator, and he was able to represent the needs of those within his administration. Like Adam, we are positioned within the earth to rule over, administer, and make intercession to God. Men are, therefore, influential in God's framework of leadership, and this helps to explain the reason our enemy, the devil, seeks to devalue us through acts of low self-esteem, suicide, immorality, identity redefinition, gender reconstruction, poor intrapersonal relationships, leave from prayer, division, and lack of appetite for the word.

The thief's purpose is to steal and kill and destroy.

My purpose is to give them a rich and satisfying life.

(John 10:10)

Declarations:

Write your name on the lines as a sign of agreement.

1) I ______________________________ will not or will no longer struggle with low self-esteem. I am valuable.

2) I______________________________ will not be the victim of suicide. I am valuable.

3) I ______________________________will not wilfully partake in any form of immorality. I am valuable.

4) I __________________________________is strong, wise, intelligent, ***(fill the space below with adjectives to describe yourself)*** ______________________________ God made me wonderful.

5) I ____________________________________ is a man. I am complete. I was carefully constructed by God. He is perfect and therefore I am perfectly designed.

6) I____________________________________ was created love all people. I will.

7) I _______________________________________commits to regularly engage in prayer.

8) I_______________________________________ resents division. I will speak constructively. I will give myself for the uniting of the believers.

9) I ____ pledge to read God's Word and continuously apply it to my life.

Let us now examine the second phrase shared by John: *"Boys do not throw stones at empty trees."*

We grew up in a rural community in Jamaica. At the time we did not have access to snacks as kids in our current world. Our only snack during the summer came from the fresh green vegetation along the countryside. We would hunt mangoes, guineps, June plums, apples, guavas, and avocados. During our many conquests, we would never climb an empty tree. We considered it a waste of time to invest in a tree that lacked the potential to yield a return. Like us boys, we are constantly exposed to the enemy's ploys as he, who once was a resident of heaven, knows first-hand what blessing awaits us. His mission is to prevent us from encountering a meaningful fellowship with God and our fellow men.

Stay alert! Watch out for your great enemy, the devil. He prowls around like a roaring lion, looking for someone to devour.

(1 Peter 5:8)

IOBI

Declarations:

I will remain focused on the mark. I refuse to be distracted by the adversary. I renounce any passion for worldly pleasure as I am conscious that these serve as paths of detours from God's will.

Do not love this world nor the things it offers you, for when you love the world, you do not have the love of the Father in you.

(1 John 2:15)

Maintaining Value is an ongoing process. Several factors are working to inflate your value, but you must adopt the appropriate principles to raise that value continuously. Paul encouraged Timothy, a younger man, to invest in his interaction with his fellow man.

Don't let anyone think less of you because you are young. Be an example to all believers in what you say, in the way you live, in your love, your faith, and your purity. ***(1 Timothy 4:12)***

Value is affected by the scarcity of an item. Paul encouraged Timothy to contend for his faith. There is a tendency to think that we must fit in with society's changing standards and, as a result, constantly alter to fit the demands of a hungry society. Where there is an influx of items, the value declines. Our value inclines when we embrace our uniqueness and employ varying methodologies to develop ourselves while pursuing our purpose in God. Timothy was encouraged to aspire for two qualities: to be an example of the believer in words and conversation. As men, we should practice a strict budget regarding the words we share and how much we disseminate.

"Every time we have to speak, we are auditioning for leadership"- *James Humes*

Declaration:

- I will ensure that the words I speak are constructive in nature.

Value can be improved by becoming a steward of:

Time: The gift of time is a precious commodity God has given man that must be utilised optimally. Time lost cannot be regained or redeemed. Man must make the best use of every opportunity presented to add value to the lives of others by investing in them what God has deposited in him. It takes time to apply oneself to increase his value. How you utilise your time will determine whether your value appreciates or depreciates.

So, teach us to number our days, that we may apply our hearts unto wisdom. ***(Psalms 90:12)***

Service: The contribution level to people's development is a clear indication of your worth/value to the organisation. It is virtually only possible to deliver with first having received. You must be served before being engaged in service. You must be committed to the task on hand to derive maximum benefit. It is God that determines your worth, and so determines your assignment. Equipping is an ongoing process that requires both the training and deployment of individuals. Service is at the core of all interpersonal relationships. In describing the worth of leaders, Jesus emphasises that the one who serves is greater than the one being served. To serve demonstrates value or worth. The emphasis of service is to add value to the life of those being served. Man will always derive value from his work or what he does—the creator God gave man work to demonstrate his worth in the garden of Eden. The greatest sense of worth is derived from knowing that you have made an invaluable contribution or investment in the lives of others.

Now these are the gifts Christ gave to the church: the apostles, the prophets, the evangelists, and the pastors and teachers. Their responsibility is to equip God's people to do his work and build up the church, the body of Christ. This will continue until we all come to such unity in our faith and knowledge of God's Son that we will be mature in the Lord, measuring up to the full and complete standard of Christ. ***(Ephesians 4:11-13)***

And whosoever will be chief among you, let him be your servant: Even as the Son of man came not to be ministered unto, but to minister, and to give his life a ransom for many. ***(John 13: 28)***

Income: Your success depends on your application of the word of God to your life. Income is based on investing time, talent, and resources to receive returns. Everyone in this world is born with the potential to realise or fulfil their purpose, and when consciously applied, that innate ability can generate income streams. A sense of self-worth is derived from being productive as we engage and empower others in income-generating endeavours. Doing this increases the value that others bring to the table. Income is directly proportional to the quality and quantity of investment.

Remember the Lord your God. He is the one who gives you power to be successful, to fulfil the covenant, he confirmed to your ancestors with an oath. ***(Deuteronomy 8:18)***

"The true worth of a man is not to be found in man himself, but in the colours and textures that come alive in others."

\- *Albert Schweitze*

Affirmations:

- I will assess my actions to ensure they are not motivated by my feelings but God's leading.

- I will submit to God's will and plan for my life rejecting the urge to live according to my own will.

- I am God's valuable representative.

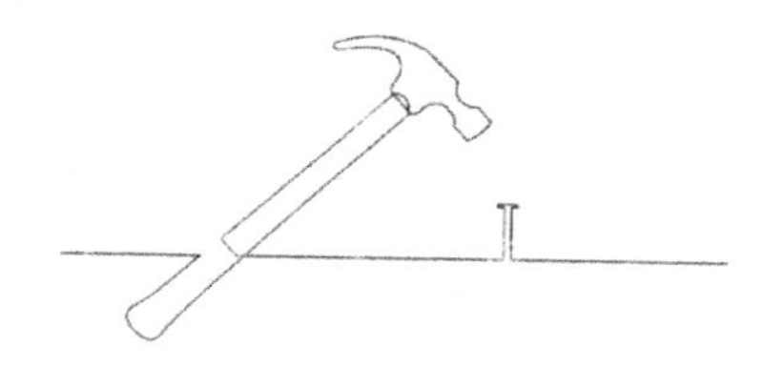

MAN, AND HIS EGO

The main task of the spirit is to free man from his ego.

Albert Einstein

People are generally quick to point out when a man is overly confident and only seeks to satisfy his ego. They skilfully blame the man's ego for every malpractice and sign of narcissism. After all, it is his fault that he has an ego and needs to rid himself of it immediately.

Such unkind accusations sometimes rob the most optimistic man of an opportunity to freely express his thoughts for fear of being described as one who is self-centred with an exaggerated sense of self-importance, or an individual marked by or characteristic of excessive admiration of or infatuation with himself. This may account for one of the reasons contributing to the high-level mental disorder among men, leading to the increased reservation and deafening silence. The inability of a man to find a safe space to express himself could be the main factor leading to his general withdrawal. It is well-known that men want to be celebrated and treated as kings for the simplest accomplishments, which boosts their confidence and promotes self-worth and fulfilment. A man or boy nurtured within a welcoming community is often upbeat, happy, and goal oriented. Support tells him that there is absolutely nothing he cannot achieve and no height he cannot ascend to.

The more we shut down our boys and men, the more we harm them mentally. He will struggle to define his worth when there is increased bad debt (inability to express himself). This is repayment he might not be able to free himself of, and as such, he becomes a victim of socialisation. His behaviour can replicate, damaging every other generation to come.

We must therefore examine the full extent of impact to which society's actions have on the man's ego. To accomplish this, we explore a suitable definition for the term ego and how it affects a man.

Psychologists and Psychotherapists describe the ego as the 'self.' Ego is from a Latin word that translates as 'I.' The ego is that aspect of the mind responsible for acting as the 'mediator' between the forces and drives of the superego; that is, our conscience, our ideal selves, and our ids, which is the part of the mind responsible for satisfying our basic needs. It operates and is also responsible for mediating between our needs and how to satisfy them within our environments. The ego maintains relations with others, reconciling the drives of the id and the superego with the outside world. Therefore, the male ego reflects not merely the individual self but also cultural definitions of masculinity and ideas about how men should think and act. Humans are social beings, and social influences shape a man's identity.

A well-known top cop, when quizzed on the appropriateness of his crime-fighting methodologies, shared this statement "show me your friend, and I will tell you who you are." The cop believed in deciding whether to make an arrest or include an individual in a criminal investigation based on the company the individual shared. He posits that people are often shaped by the environment in which they live and the people they interact with. Our thoughts and conduct are socially constructed. For example, a man may grow up thinking it is quite appropriate to have several "baby mothers" because it is generally accepted by society and thus empowers him within circles. Such a man has been cultured to consider this deportment as an act of prestige. He is affected by his society and will find it difficult to live outside of that social construct.

He embraces this behaviour as the way of life and as, subsequently, will find it difficult to do otherwise.

For as he thinketh in his heart, so is he. ***(Proverbs 23:7 a)***

You are the total product of your thoughts, and if the immoral world shapes those thoughts, you will also be unprincipled. This is why the 'well-built' man must renew his thinking and align them with the ways of God. As we are developed, we must actively engage in a cyclical process that seeks to create positive environments for men to be empowered and actualised. We must become the role models of tomorrow's generation today, always endeavouring to harvest and disseminate good social skills. Additionally, we should rid ourselves of negative thinking that ultimately leads to misbehaviour.

Don't copy the behaviour and customs of this world, but let God transform you into a new person by changing the way you think. Then you will learn to know God's will for you, which is good and pleasing and perfect. ***(Romans 12:2)***

We have the power to shape our thoughts even in changing circumstances. Therefore, we are not victims of societal norms or biological robots wired to execute prompts from command scripts. Furthermore, we are not bound to submit to the views and opinions of rock stars and other persons of influence, and we are in control of our thoughts as the complete authority over our own path.

"An uncontrolled ego will, without a shadow of a doubt, turn you into a selfish person – or even worse makes you 'egocentric' which has disastrous effects on your overall development and your quest for a more fulfilling life." - *Unknown*

Reflection:

Write down FIVE Positive thoughts that you will embrace today.

1. ____

____

____

2. ____

____

____

3. ____

____

____

4. ____

____

____

5. ____

____

____

Dr. Caroline Leaf's book, Switch on Your Brain opines, "As we think, we change the physical nature of our brain. As we consciously direct our thinking, we can wire out toxic thinking patterns and replace them with healthy thoughts."

We are uniquely created with the ability to choose. We are, therefore, shareholders in our destiny. We must decide to encounter God's blessings for our families and us. Moral and ethical thoughts are the springboard for conscious decisions.

Today I have given you the choice between life and death, between blessings and curses. Now I call on heaven and earth to witness the choice you make. Oh, that you would choose life, so that you and your descendants might live!

(Deuteronomy 30:19)

Ethical thoughts give life to hope, rekindle faith, and build trust. These are the benefits of a restored mind. How can my thoughts be restored?

Thoughts are transformed through:

Our Honest Prayer to God.

Express to God your weakness and ask him to renew your thinking. The Bible shares an account of King David in which his own thinking led him to commit adultery, plotting and orchestrating the death of his own soldier and then taking his wife to be his wife. Can you imagine how his thoughts may have affected him? You can cover up or hide your deeds from another person but cannot hide from yourself. It may have been more uncomfortable for David than a season of comfort. Damaged and messed up thinking can lead to stress, depression, poor decisions, job loss, eating disorders, and even suicide. One must seek to purge his thoughts immediately. We, too, are often led away to participate in acts that displease God. The Guilt and shame of our actions act as persecutors, constantly reminding us of our flaws and calling for condemnation. This is the basis for a renewed mind with immediate effect. David eventually prayed.

Don't keep looking at my sins. Remove the stain of my guilt. Create in me a clean heart, O God. Renew a loyal spirit within me. Do not banish me from your presence, and don't take your Holy Spirit from me. Restore to me the joy of your salvation and make me willing to obey you. ***(Psalms 51:9-12)***

Let us Pray:

Dear Lord,
Pardon me of all my errors. Renew my mind from the guilt and grant me positive thoughts.
Amen.

Study of God's Word.

The Bible is the most effective resource on the earth, capable of reminding you of the truth. It is fitted to God's thoughts towards humanity; therefore, it is necessary to feed your spirit on the word of God.

Work hard so you can present yourself to God and receive his approval. Be a good worker, one who does not need to be ashamed and who correctly explains the word of truth.

(2 Timothy 2:15)

Reflection:

Repeat this for next seven days!

God's Word has tremendous benefits. It:

- **Sanctifies.**

Make them holy by your truth; teach them your word, which is truth. **(John 17:17)**

- **Works Effectively.**

Therefore, we never stop thanking God that when you received his message from us, you did not think of our words as mere human ideas. You accepted what we said as the very word of God—which, of course, it is. And this word continues to work on you who believe.

- **Come With the Power of The Holy Spirit**.

When we brought you the Good News, it was not only with words but also with power, for the Holy Spirit assured you that what we said was true. And you know our concern for you from how we lived with you. **(1 Thessalonians 1:5)**

- **Builds Faith.**

So, faith comes from hearing, that is, hearing the Good News about Christ. **(Romans 10:17)**

- **Reminds You of Your Identity.**

But you are not like that, for you are a chosen people. You are royal priests, a holy nation, God's very own possession. As a result, you can show others the goodness of God, for he called you out of the darkness into his wonderful light. **(1 Peter 2:9)**

May your mind be fully transformed today bearing the very mind of God.

Let this mind be in you, which was also in Christ Jesus.

(Philippians 2:5)

Affirmations:

- I will avoid asking why my life is the way it is and start asking what God is teaching me and how I can submit to His guidance.

- I will remove the mental filter that causes psychosocial distortion in how I see myself as a man.

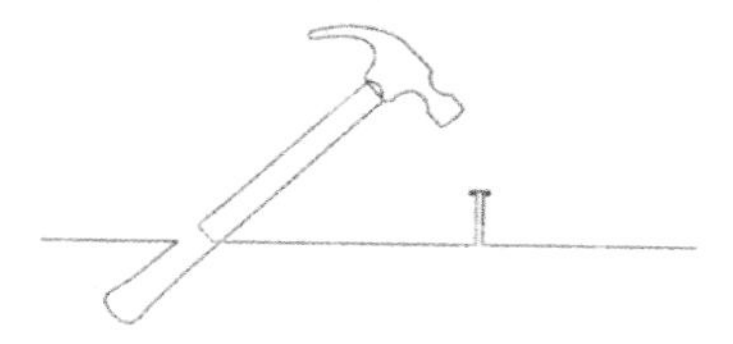

THE MAN'S ACTIVITY:

S	H	A	R	E	H	O	L	D	E	R
S	N	U	P	R	E	M	E	W	E	J
N	E	L	M	G	E	S	A	D	G	C
I	A	C	A	A	I	G	L	L	R	M
N	Y	N	R	G	N	O	A	E	E	H
E	A	S	N	U	H	B	A	M	A	Y
M	L	A	H	E	O	T	E	H	I	A
P	M	A	K	R	I	S	S	I	D	M
R	V	A	M	O	W	H	E	A	N	N
K	T	Y	N	E	S	M	M	R	K	G
S	Y	L	B	I	F	L	M	Q	N	K

Adam
Human Being
Man
Male
Female
Ishshah
Iysh

Creation
Plan
Design
Manage
Image
Resources
Shareholder
Stakeholder

REFERENCES

Bandura, A. (1977). Social learning theory. Englewood Cliffs, NJ: Prentice Hall.

https://www.baltimoremagazine.com/section/health/how-does-love-affect-your-well-being/

https://www.betterhelp.com/advice/love/7-reasons-why-love-and-sex-go-together/

http://psychology.iresearchnet.com/social-psychology/control/modeling-of-behavior/

https://www.drjamesdobson.org/blogs/jt-waresak/5things-man-must-know-lead-his-family

Weinreich, Peter (1986). "14: The operationalisation of identity theory in racial and ethnic relations". In Rex, John; Mason, David (eds.). *Theories of Race and Ethnic Relations*. Comparative Ethnic and Race Relations. Cambridge: Cambridge University Press (published 1988). pp. 299ff. ISBN 9780521369398. Retrieved 2018-08-30.

ABOUT THE AUTHOR

Nicholas A Robertson (Director)

NICHOLAS A. ROBERTSON, Dip. Min (Hon.), Dip.Ed. (Hon.), BD (Hon.) B. Ed (Hon.) M.Ed. (Hon.) is a dynamic speaker, counsellor, mentor, and educator who meticulously uses his expertise from military service and his pedagogy to expound on the principles of the Kingdom of God. From as early as 2006, he has been actively involved in ministry and his service transcends borders. To date, he has served in Jamaica, the United States of America, and the United Kingdom. Rev Robertson has operated in the following areas: Youth Ministry, Evangelism, Christian Education, Leadership, Radio, and Social Media ministry.

He studied at the Church Teacher's College, University of the West Indies, Mona, United Theological College of the West Indies, and the Christian Leaders College.

He is the founder of Positive Vibration 365 Plus Global, a daily devotional on social media; co-host of Mr. & Mrs. Robdon's Couples Corner and is also the founder and COO of BuildAMan Foundation Global., a non-profit initiative to develop Godly men, husbands, and fathers. He is also co-founder and director of Impact Online Bible Institute Ltd. He is also the author of Positive Vibration: Navigating through Difficult Times, a book towards equipping persons with the appropriate attitude to navigate life's journey. He is also the author of Positive Vibration: Biblical Keys for Faith Activation. Additionally, he co-authors Critical Keys for Biblical Interpretation: The Believer's Handbook (Book 1 and Book 2)

Nicholas 'Robdon' Robertson is married to Danielle Robertson and they both share two beautiful children: Danick and Danice.

ABOUT THE AUTHOR

Valentine Rodney (Deputy Director)

REV. VALENTINE A. RODNEY, BSc, MA. is an international speaker whose ministry has taken him to the USA, Canada, Europe, Africa, and several countries within the Caribbean, where he has also fostered and facilitated ministerial developmental programmes. He has done undergraduate work at the University of the West Indies in Marine Biology and Graduate work in Missions at the Caribbean Graduate School of Theology. Rev. Rodney has served in the areas of Christian Education, Evangelism, Leadership Development, Prayer and Intercession, Youth Ministry, Radio and Television and Pastorate. He is also actively involved in welfare programmes and mentorship to men, youths, and ministers. He is a strong advocate for Christian Transformational Development where the church interfaces with the community and assists in strategic intervention that is both redemptive and empowering.

He is the author of the books, Shameless Persistence the Audacity of Purposeful Praying, La Persistencia Desvergonzada: La Audacia de la Oración con Propósito and The Power of the Secret Place; the place of relationship, resolution, and revelation and has co-authored Critical Keys for Biblical Interpretation: The Believers Handbook (1&2).

Rev. Rodney is an International Instructor for Walk Thru The Bible Ministries, Co-founder and Deputy Director of Impact Online Bible Institute (IOBI), and the Director of Word Impact Ministries International, a non-denominational ministry that caters to the empowerment of the Christian Community and the salvation of the lost. He is an International Chaplain and Ambassador with Covenant International University and Seminary. His Motto is *"Go where there is no path and leave a trail."* VALENTINE A. RODNEY is married to Yevett for twenty-four years and their union has produced two daughters, Zharia and Ana-Olivia.

CONTRIBUTING AUTHOR

Danielle Brown-Robertson (Admin Director)

DANIELLE BROWN-ROBERTSON, BA (Hon.), Post Grad Dip is a dynamic speaker and Educator. Being the child of ministers, she became actively involved in the church in her teenage years and later pursued theological studies at the United Theological College of the West Indies. Prior to migrating to the US, Danielle served as youth minister and administrative secretary for the United Church in Jamaica and the Cayman Islands. Due to her love for nurturing young minds, she completed teacher training at UWI and worked in the middle school classroom in the US. On migrating to the UK, Danielle made a bold decision to decline her teaching role and support the Kingdom inspired vision, Positive

Vibration. She is currently the weekly host of the morning program and co-host of Mr and Mrs Robdon Couples' Corner. Along with her husband she leads a family vlog on YouTube called the **'THE ROBDONS'** where they provide useful tips on marriage, finances, and family. She has dedicated her time to advance the vision.

Danielle is the wife of Nicholas A Robertson and the mother of two beautiful children, Danick and Danice.

CONTRIBUTOR

Ontonio Dawson (Guest writer)

Ontonio Dawson is a devoted Minister of Religion and the founder of a weekly devotional programme called "Spiritual Breakfast Network", established in 2014. His audio devotional messages started out WhatsApp and has reached people globally. He has not expanded the ministry and his message can be found on his website, YouTube, and Facebook. He is also a content creator on Facebook and his videos has reached thousands of people. Ontonio is also the founder of the **#SpeakBlackMan** Movement which aims to educate and empower males about mental health difficulties, encourage them to speak about their emotion and guide them to make practical changes in their life using psychological techniques to manage and overcome mental health challenges.

BECOME A STUDENT AT IOBI

We are a subsidiary organization of the Positive Vibration Global group of ministries dedicated to providing training to the community equipping them to serve areas of ministry within the marketplace.

We offer flexible and affordable tailored to you or your church's demand. These include six weeks courses, webinars, accelerated program, training and support programs, life coaching, leadership, and empowerment programs.

Our courses are thoroughly researched and prepared with you in mind.

Follow the link to register: https://bit.ly/IOBIRegistration

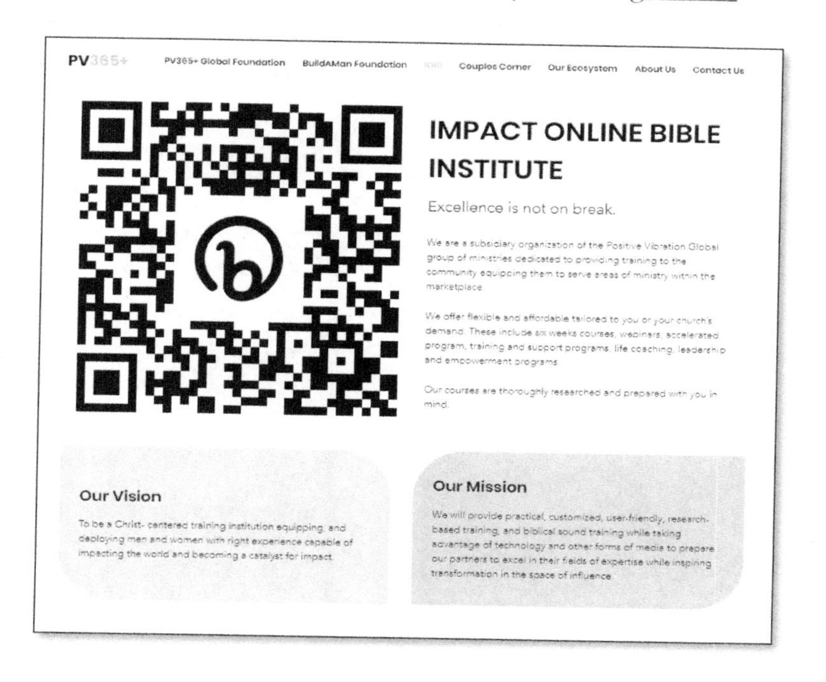

ADDITIONAL RESOURCE

Check out our books from varying categories:

Faith, discipline and growth:

Enduring difficult times

Building Thriving Marriage s:

Building Thriving Marriages:

Leadership, Administration and Management:

Creating Financial Freedom.

Discipleship, Evangelism, Missions:

Youth empowerment and mentorship

Purpose, Vision, Leadership, Men Empowerment:

Creating Intimacy in marriage.

Tools for interpreting the Bible:

Tools for interpreting the Bible:

Prayer, reflection, and meditation:

Prayer, reflection, and meditation:

Prayer, reflection, and meditation:

Prayer, reflection, and meditation:

Notes

- ✓ **Visit our website to order Sign Copies: https://www.positivevibrationglobal.com/shop**
- ✓ Also available on Amazon and Barnes & Noble
- ✓ Contact us on Facebook @Impact Online Bible Institute
- ✓ Email: nrobertson@positivevibrationglobal.com

Printed in Great Britain
by Amazon